4 -13

brilliant

self
confidence

PEARSON

At Pearson, we take learning personally. Our courses and resources are available as books, online and via multi-lingual packages, helping people learn whatever, wherever and however they choose.

We work with leading authors to develop the strongest learning experiences, bringing cutting-edge thinking and best learning practice to a global market. We craft our print and digital resources to do more to help learners not only understand their content, but to see it in action and apply what they learn, whether studying or at work.

Pearson is the world's leading learning company. Our portfolio includes Penguin, Dorling Kindersley, the Financial Times and our educational business, Pearson International. We are also a leading provider of electronic learning programmes and of test development, processing and scoring services to educational institutions, corporations and professional bodies around the world.

Every day our work helps learning flourish, and wherever learning flourishes, so do people.

To learn more please visit us at: **www.pearson.com/uk**

self confidence

second edition

How to challenge your fears and go for anything you want in life

Mike McClement

PEARSON

Harlow, England • London • New York • Boston • San Francisco • Toronto • Sydney • Auckland • Singapore • Hong Kong
Tokyo • Seoul • Taipei • New Delhi • Cape Town • São Paulo • Mexico City • Madrid • Amsterdam • Munich • Paris • Milan

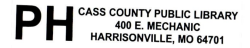

PEARSON EDUCATION LIMITED

Edinburgh Gate
Harlow CM20 2JE
Tel: +44 (0)1279 623623
Fax: +44 (0)1279 431059
Website: www.pearson.com/uk

First published 2010 (print)
Second edition published 2012 (print and electronic)

Pearson Education is not responsible for the content of third party internet sites.

ISBN: 978-1-4479-2959-8 (print)
       978-1-4479-2973-4 (PDF)
       978-0-273-77832-5 (ePub)

British Library Cataloguing-in-Publication Data
A catalog record for the print edition is available from the British Library

Library of Congress Cataloging-in-Publication Data
A catalog record for the print edition is available from the Library of Congress

10 9 8 7 6 5 4 3 2 1
16 15 14 13 12

Print edition typeset in 10/14pt Plantin by 3
Printed in Great Britain by Henry Ling Ltd., at the Dorset Press, Dorchester,
Dorset

NOTE THAT ANY PAGE REFERENCES REFER TO THE PRINT
EDITION

Contents

About the author   vii
Acknowledgements   ix
Introduction   xi

part 1 Engaging your positive mindset   1

  1 Are you born with self-confidence?   3
  2 Being and feeling more positive   33
  3 Knowing what you want to achieve   53

part 2 Communicating with self-confidence   67

  4 How do people see you?   69
  5 How do you communicate?   91

part 3 Putting self-confidence into action   109

  6 Why is assertiveness so important?   111
  7 Showing true confidence, verbally and non-verbally   151
  8 Confidence at home and at work   179

part 4 Keeping up the momentum   215

  9 Dealing with setbacks   217
 10 Using your new-found self-confidence to really
     change your life   227

     Conclusion: Following it through   243
     Index   246

About the author

Mike McClement has over 20 years' experience in the field of personal development. His particular interest and motivation lies in the challenge of helping people to realise their full potential and make the most of their lives.

He founded *Training Hand Ltd* in 1995 and, more recently, its sister company *Think Confidence*. Both companies focus on the provision of personal development training and coaching.

Mike's professional expertise is in the areas of self-confidence, assertiveness, motivation and personal effectiveness. His work centres around the development and facilitation of bespoke training for groups and, on a more personal level, one-to-one coaching programmes for individuals. He also delivers speeches and short workshops on confidence and motivation at business events and conferences.

In business, he works in both the public and private sectors and at all levels of seniority, from chief executive to junior staff member. His courses are also popular with people who need to build their confidence in their personal lives outside work.

Mike lives in Devon, UK with his wife and three teenage children. He's a keen tennis player and skier and keeps fit running on the coastal trails of south-east Devon.

He can be contacted by email:

mike@thinkconfidence.com

 Join Mike on LinkedIn

Follow Mike on Twitter

Find Mike's blog at mikemcclement.blogspot.com

Join Think Confidence on Facebook

Acknowledgements

My thanks go to all who've helped me with this second edition. In particular, my wife, Jenny, for all the support she's given and for her hard work and expertise in creating and running the **www.thinkconfidence.com** website. Thank you also to my children, Madeleine, Toby and Anna, for being patient with me.

Lastly, huge thanks to all the people whose experiences are mentioned in the text. Although their names have been changed, as with the first edition, it wouldn't have been possible to write the book without reference to real people who have struggled with confidence and succeeded in overcoming their difficulties. I thank them all and wish them luck for the future.

Introduction

Visualise it to believe it, practise it to become it ...

In the first edition of *Brilliant Confidence*, I told a true story about Sid, my neighbour. It took Sid eighteen months to build his own house. I kept track of his progress. Mostly he worked alone, just occasionally he needed help. I remember watching him look up at his house and walk proudly through the front door when he'd finished. Sid knew what he wanted his house to look like; he had a plan and he achieved it. Brick by brick, Sid had built his house.

It wasn't until after he'd finished that he told me he'd never built a house before!

Pretty impressive! Sid started from scratch but wasn't daunted by the task ahead. He knew the size of his challenge but he didn't let it frighten him. You too have a challenge ahead; think of it as your *Self-Confidence Project*. My neighbour built his house; you're going to build your self-confidence. Sid is a great role model. You'll need to take the same approach as he did. It might not take you eighteen months but it's not going to happen overnight.

Sid's self-confidence was sky high after he'd finished his house. In fact, he's built two more houses since then! I've seen them; they too are very impressive. But it hasn't all been plain sailing for Sid. He's had his ups and downs. He's made some mistakes too.

I know this because he's told me. He's learnt from these mistakes, stayed positive and moved on. He's building his fourth house now.

It's going to be the same for you as your self-confidence project unfolds. You'll definitely have your ups and downs, you'll make mistakes too. That's natural, that's to be expected. Sid learnt from his mistakes and that's exactly what you'll have to do.

Don't worry, don't panic! I'm not trying to frighten you off! I'm just preparing you for the challenge ahead. Your self-confidence project will be incredibly rewarding if you commit to it. If you *really* want it to, it will change your life.

What you visualise, you believe and what you practise, you become. This is so true. Sid had a picture of how he wanted his house to look. He knew what he was aiming for. You'll need to visualise yourself as a confident person, doing the things that confident people do; if you do this, you'll know what you're aiming for. Once you know this, you practise, practise, practise … and practise some more. This is how you learn. It's how everyone who's good at what they do learns: athletes, sports stars, good presenters, chief executives, actors, builders like Sid and, of course, confident people.

You'll need self-discipline and energy. You'll need courage too, yes *courage*, to attempt the things you didn't think you could do. At times you'll feel frustrated and at other times you'll feel emotional. Don't give up, never give up; keep persevering and, step-by-step, your self-confidence, self-belief and self-esteem will grow.

Think back over the last few weeks and months. How many times have you lacked the self-confidence to do something you *know* you should have done? Something that would have helped you; something that was right for you; something, perhaps, that you would have enjoyed? Or how many times have you not spoken up when you knew you were right?

If you're honest with yourself, the answer to these questions will probably be 'quite a few'. That's because very few people have the self-confidence, self-belief and self-discipline to do the right thing all the time.

Brilliant Self Confidence builds on the first edition and is a practical and logical no-nonsense solution to dealing with confidence issues. It reinforces the key points and breaks into new territory. It relates directly to the reality of life. It can be applied to your work life, your social life and your home life.

This second edition also looks in more detail at how to achieve more through personal objective setting, how to overcome self-doubt and how to come to terms with and deal with setbacks along the way. I've also incorporated a handy summary at the end of each chapter. The text's full of practical advice and examples of how real people have overcome their lack of confidence or self-esteem; real people who have made real changes to their lives.

Get ready though – the text will challenge you. It will invite you to reflect and it will make you think. You'll learn things about yourself that you didn't know, things perhaps that you didn't think were important.

The text is linked to the **www.thinkconfidence.com** website. Here you'll find links to other reading material. There are also questionnaires you can complete to learn more about yourself and your confidence levels in relation to the way you communicate and deal with conflict. You can even take the 'Think Confidence Reality Check' which invites others to give you feedback on *their* perception of you in terms of your confidence, communication style and assertiveness.

In short, by using the techniques addressed in the text, you'll develop the self-confidence to overcome your fears, seize opportunities, speak up when required, enjoy yourself and live life to the full.

PART 1

Engaging your positive mindset

CHAPTER 1

Are you born with self-confidence?

'm going to be honest with you. Sometimes I feel confident and sometimes I don't. OK, I admit it ...

Hold on, you're probably thinking! I'm reading a book about self-confidence written by someone who isn't confident! Well, you're kind of right – but don't panic, there's nothing to worry about. The truth is that even confident people doubt themselves and struggle with self-confidence on occasions. The fact is, we're all human and sometimes things just don't go according to plan.

So just to set your mind at ease, overall, I *would* describe myself as a confident person. That's because I've learnt how to deal with the times when my confidence levels are at their lowest. I've accepted that life isn't all plain sailing. I've also realised that I'm the one who controls how the 'down' times affect me.

Born lucky?

Some people struggle with self-confidence because they think they're unlucky. These people are convinced that confident people are lucky because they were born confident.

This just isn't true.

The first thing to accept about self-confidence is that at birth we're all born on a level playing field. We all start together at the same point on the path to self-confidence. If you continue to think you're at a disadvantage to confident people because you weren't born confident, then the playing field that used to be level will turn into a steeper and steeper upward slope.

So, before you read on, it's important to come to terms with this and *believe* it.

Confident people aren't *born* confident. Self-confidence is an attitude that develops. It might be worth taking a few seconds to mull this over. Some people accept it but don't really believe it. If you don't believe it, it will become a convenient excuse. It then becomes a heavy burden that hinders you whenever you find yourself outside your comfort zone.

> confident people aren't *born* confident

Controlling your state of mind, thinking positively and *believing* that you can change for the better is one of the first steps on the road to increased self-confidence. If you know how to approach this challenge, you'll succeed ... and that's what *Brilliant Self Confidence* is all about. Success.

Try thinking of confidence as a *skill* that relates to your attitude and your state of mind. It isn't something concrete or something of substance that you can touch or put your finger on, but it is tangible. So if it's a skill, you can learn it. Think back to other skills you've learnt as your life has moved on, for example reading, writing, riding a bike, or driving a car, and treat confidence in the same way.

Remember, you can acquire self-confidence at any stage in your life. You can *learn* how to feel and look more confident as you grow and mature. Everyone can do this. We all have the opportunity to build our self-confidence as our lives move on.

 **brilliant tip**

No one is born with confidence; it is a skill which we can all learn.

What's your problem with confidence?

Let's get straight to the point. Why are you reading *Brilliant Self Confidence?* You'll have your own personal reasons. Some people are faced with a specific hurdle in their lives which they can't overcome because they lack self-confidence. Others are struggling with a number of issues relating to confidence, self-belief or self-esteem. Or perhaps you're one of the people who doesn't feel they have any major issues to address but simply sees confidence as an essential 'life-skill' that successful people learn.

Whatever your reasons, if you answer 'yes' to any of these questions, *Brilliant Self Confidence* will focus your mind and present solutions.

Would you like to be able to:

	Yes/No	
• Seize opportunities before they pass you by?	☐	☐
• Speak up when you know you're right?	☐	☐
• Feel comfortable and in control when you walk into a room of people you don't know?	☐	☐
• Be more assertive and influential?	☐	☐
• Overcome and use to positive effect the nerves you might feel when speaking in public?	☐	☐
• Present your thoughts clearly and confidently even when you fear the person may disagree with you?	☐	☐
• Introduce yourself confidently and charismatically at social events and work meetings?	☐	☐
• Wake up every morning and feel motivated and clear about what you aim to achieve from the day ahead, both at work and in your personal life?	☐	☐
• Boost your self-esteem and overcome any negative perceptions that are holding you back?	☐	☐

You're not unusual if you struggle with some of these things on occasions. Far from it, you're normal. In fact you'd be unusual if you *didn't* struggle because these are everyday challenges that we all face.

The list may look pretty daunting. Now you've read it, perhaps you're thinking to yourself: 'I can't be … because I'm not …' or 'I couldn't possibly behave like … because I don't have …'

It's critical that you dispel these negative thoughts. Try to see your Self-Confidence Project as the catalyst to this new, more positive and courageous way of thinking.

We often think these negative thoughts because we doubt ourselves. Self-doubt is a natural phenomenon we all experience from time to time so don't think you're any different to others. Confident people experience this too but their self-belief and self-discipline override this feeling of doubt; they don't let it stop them trying new ways of thinking and behaving. It takes courage to do this.

What's behind self-doubt?

'Our doubts are traitors, and make us lose the good we oft might win, by fearing to attempt.'

William Shakespeare, *Measure for Measure, 1604.*

Self-doubt arises for many reasons, some explicable and completely understandable, others with no apparent explanation. Self-doubt is destructive; it will hold you back if you can't overcome it. So let's dispel some of the misconceptions that exist about confidence that help to explain why self-doubt arises. Try to banish these misconceptions right now if they're hindering you and fuelling your self-doubt.

Common misconceptions about self-confidence

Misconception – Self-confidence comes naturally to talented people

It's a fact that some people are naturally more talented at some things than others. For example, some people are naturally more gifted at sport than others. It's also true that some people are gifted with high intelligence, others can sing well, others are good dancers, others are gifted with creativity and so on.

So, yes, there are indeed natural talents that we're born with. However, it doesn't automatically follow that a naturally talented person is a confident person.

There are some people who seem to exude confidence naturally. Think of people you see on television; people who perform to an audience of millions. This would seem an absolutely impossible task to the majority of us and you would probably think that someone who can perform in front of such large audiences couldn't possibly have problems with confidence. You'd be wrong. For example, in his biography write-up by Dominic Wills, Mickey Rourke is described as headstrong and opinionated but always lacking in self-confidence. And Robbie Williams admitted having problems with confidence when he performed on *The X Factor* and even Gary Barlow has talked about how low his self-esteem was when Take That originally broke up. The truth is that, no matter how talented you are, you can still suffer from a lack of confidence or self-esteem.

The key is to be satisfied in your own abilities and to know that you're giving your best. The way to make this work is to accept that what's important is what *you* think, not what others think about you.

Don't doubt yourself if you think you lack talent. Try to harness the skills that you have. We all have strengths. It's what *you* think that matters, not what others think.

Misconception – You have to be good-looking or popular to be confident

You'll need to get this out of your mind. Your looks should not interfere with your confidence levels. Think about people you know who you would describe as confident. I'll bet the majority of them don't look like Brad Pitt or Angelina Jolie, do they? In fact – would you describe *any* of them as good-looking? Maybe one or two perhaps, but you'd expect that with the law of averages.

The key here is that it's not what you look like physically that's important. It's your self-belief and how you feel on the inside that forms the nucleus of self-confidence.

It doesn't matter what you look like. Your looks will have *no* impact on your confidence levels unless you let them.

Misconception – Confidence is all about your physical presence

It's true that presenting yourself well helps if you want to come across confidently. However, you need more than just physical presence.

Physical presence and the assertive presentation of your thoughts is the last activity in a chain of events. To appear confident, every link in the chain needs to be strong. The strength of the chain and its ability to withstand stress is generated through your mindset. Having the strength of character to believe in yourself and your abilities is a critical element of the process.

Thinking positively is essential in relation to self-belief. We'll cover this and link it to ways you can develop and harness your self-belief (in Chapter 2).

> thinking positively is essential in relation to self-belief

 **brilliant** tip

Physical presence has to be supported by self-belief in order to generate self-confidence.

Misconception – Confident people can deal with situations without even thinking about them

This just isn't true. Try asking a friend you would describe as confident how it is that they manage to deal confidently with situations they aren't expecting. If you don't have a confident friend you know well enough, just watch how confident people conduct themselves. You'll come up with the same answers either way.

When dealing with an unexpected event, confident people prepare properly before they act. They don't just jump in and do or say something without thinking about it. In other words, they have the self-discipline to create *time* for themselves. Sometimes, all that's available is a few seconds – that's better than nothing. Confident people have the self-control to think about what they're going to say before they say it. There's pretty well always some time available to do this. Confident people create it and use it effectively.

> confident people have the self-control to think about what they are going to say before they say it

So, confident people don't have an in-built natural ability to deal with situations off the cuff. If necessary, they create time and think before they act.

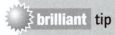 **brilliant** tip

Prepare properly before you commit. There's always time available. You just need to have the presence of mind and confidence to grab it.

Misconceptions – You need praise and appreciation from others to be confident

This isn't the case – and you should try not to let it be the case. It's nice to be appreciated and to be told you've done well or done a good job on occasions. However, it's not an essential requirement for self-confidence. It's true that some people need praise and appreciation more than others in order to feel confident. Even if you are one of these people, don't worry. If you work using personal achievement to motivate you, you'll feel less reliant on the praise and appreciation of others.

 **brilliant** tip

Try to live and work for achievement, not praise and appreciation.

Changing your attitude and approach

Now that you've dealt with these misconceptions, you should be in a stronger position to get started.

People lack confidence for many reasons. In fact I've never met two people who share the same reasons. It's quite often the case that someone's lack of confidence, self-esteem or self-belief originates from their experiences in life. Before we move on to consider how these experiences might have had an impact on you, it's helpful to reflect on how you approached life as a child.

Have you ever wondered why most young children have a natural instinct to learn? They seem to have an in-built curiosity about things they see and hear around them. In most cases, they're prepared to 'have a go' and try something out in order to satisfy this instinct. It's true that some children are naturally shy, but normally even they will eventually take a step forward and try something that interests them. Young children seem to have a natural self-belief and determination that drives a dynamo inside them. Parents will know that, on occasions, this dynamo can be so powerful that it's difficult to control!

So what's changed between then and now? Why does this dynamo that used to drive us now seem so slow? In some of us it may even have crusted up and jammed as time has moved on and we've matured. To start to feel and act more confidently, you need to get it working again.

This exercise will help to free up your dynamo.

 **exercise**

Turning the clock back

Try to think back to when you were young. Think of a time when you learnt to do something that you've never forgotten since; something that has stayed with you right up to this point in your life. This might perhaps have been when you learnt to swim, to ride a bike or to do something else significant. Now think carefully about this experience and how, as a child, you approached it.

Write down some words or phrases that would help to describe your approach and how you remember feeling about that new challenge.

Don't read on just yet – complete the list of words or phrases first.

Now bring your mind back to more recent times, to the period of time over which you feel you've lacked self-confidence. Think of a situation that ▶

stands out; a situation that involved doing or learning something new; a situation when you remember your lack of confidence letting you down. This could be to do with work or your personal life – perhaps it was an interview you went to, a presentation you gave, a party you went to or maybe an argument you had with someone.

Now do the same as before and write down some words or phrases that would help to describe your approach and how you remember feeling about this more recent event.

When you've finished, look at the two lists together – reflect on the words you've chosen to describe the two experiences. Think first about the words you've written down to describe the experience when you were young. Ask yourself what they say about your approach to the task and what they tell you about your feelings.

You've probably written down words like 'fun', 'interesting', 'challenging', 'enjoyable', 'exciting' and phrases like 'no inhibitions', 'desperate to learn' and 'couldn't wait'. You've probably also written down words like 'anxious', 'difficult', 'scary', 'dangerous', 'embarrassing', 'sore', 'tiring' and 'frustrating' and phrases like 'didn't like it', 'couldn't do it at first' and 'found it really hard'.

How do these words and phrases differ from the ones you've used to describe your more recent experience? Ask yourself what the contrasts are. Is there a main theme you can draw out that encapsulates and describes your feelings and approach to each of the experiences?

Now identify and write down the main differences between the two lists. Does anything jump out at you? It shouldn't be long before you see how your approach to the challenge when you were young differs from your more recent experience. You can learn a great deal from this.

As a child, you had no inhibitions. As a child you wanted to learn new things and to tackle new challenges, even when these challenges were quite daunting. Trying new things was exciting as a child. You had a natural motivation and curiosity. You didn't fear failure, you probably didn't even think about failing. Your natural desire to learn just took over and propelled you on. You recognised the challenge and got on with achieving it with determination.

So, in essence, the list describing your childhood experience has a more positive, enthusiastic, focused and motivated feel to it. Yes, there are probably some negative words or phrases there but the key point is that you didn't let them get in the way. They didn't stop you striving to achieve the task.

If you could do this as a child, there's no reason why you can't do the same as an adult. There should be no reason why you can't learn new skills now, just as you did when you were young. The difficulty is that as we mature, other issues start to cloud our judgement. For example, we start to wonder what others might think, we start to worry about failing, we start to question our decisions, we start to look back at our other failures and, eventually, if we lack the confidence to take a step into the unknown, we decide that it would be safer to stay as we are. Or, depending on the situation, perhaps we decide that it would be safer not to say anything, not to rock the boat, not to risk upsetting someone.

So, reflect again now on the words you wrote down to describe your more recent experience. Think about why they tend to focus more on the negatives. Why are you letting them affect your approach and your confidence levels? Try telling yourself that nothing has changed since you were young – yes, you've grown up and matured physically but, in terms of your mindset, nothing has changed. So, therefore, there's no reason why you should behave any differently. Why are you letting those things that didn't bother you then bother you now?

brilliant tip

Don't let negative attitudes or pressures affect you. Try to approach new opportunities and challenges like you did as a child.

 **brilliant** example

Sally

Sally lacked confidence. She was frustrated because she felt she was missing out on opportunities in her life. She had just moved to London and was living away from home for the first time. She was sharing a flat with an old friend from school. She wanted to make new friends and decided to take up ballroom dancing.

She did some research and found that a local hotel was organising ballroom dancing lessons on Thursday evenings. She persuaded her friend to go along too and they went for the first time. There were about 50 people there, none of whom they had met before. They spent the evening meeting new people and dancing with the guidance of an instructor, who stood on the stage and took the group through some simple moves.

Sally really enjoyed it and when they got home she told her friend she couldn't wait till next Thursday when they could go again for the next lesson. But her friend said she didn't really want to go again because she hadn't enjoyed it much. Sally was really disappointed and started to think twice about going again because she didn't want to go on her own.

Eventually, having thought about it all week, she summoned up the courage and went again the following Thursday. She hoped and prayed that some of the people she had met last time would be there again so she didn't have to meet new people on her own. To her horror though, when she walked in, she didn't recognise a soul. She spent the evening feeling really uncomfortable and eventually decided to leave early. It just hadn't been the same without her friend – whereas before she'd found it easy to meet people, this time, without her friend there for support, she really struggled.

Sally found this incredibly frustrating because she knew she loved ballroom dancing and desperately wanted to carry on. Some weeks went by without her going. Then she decided to go on a confidence-building course in the hope that she might be able to overcome her fears. On the course, she was introduced to the concept of casting your mind back. In fact, her memories were very relevant because she thought back to the ballet lessons she had had when she was about six or seven years old. She remembered how much she'd enjoyed them and how she'd approached them. She reflected on her mental attitude back then as a child and how that might help her now. She realised that she needed to set aside her fears and her shyness.

The next week, she went again on the Thursday evening. On the way, she made a point of remembering how she'd found it so easy to relax into the situation when she was younger. With these memories at the forefront of her mind, she walked through the door at the start and thought positively about the whole experience. She forgot her inhibitions.

As a result she thoroughly enjoyed it. She hadn't known anyone when she walked in but had made four new dancing friends by the end.

---

brilliant tip

Think back to your attitude to learning new skills as a child. Try to set aside your inhibitions like you used to.

Learning from your experiences and those who influenced you

Childhood

So far, in relation to casting your mind back, we've talked in general terms about your attitude and how you can change it for the better by reflecting on how you used to approach new situations when you were young. Feelings like fear and anxiety just didn't exist then.

There are other lessons we can learn from thinking back. Have a look at these examples of people who've benefited by rewinding the clock back to their childhood. Do they ring any bells?

 **example**

Miles

Miles, a 37-year-old accountant, was a shy person who had spent the majority of his adult life, in his words, 'lacking confidence and belief in myself'. I explained to him that it might help to reflect on his experiences to see if he could remember any specific events that had affected his confidence levels. He tried this but couldn't remember anything in particular.

So I asked him about his childhood. Again, there was nothing he could remember about his childhood that stood out. In fact he described his childhood as 'normal, fun and loving'. Probing just a little, I asked him about his parents and how they brought him up. It was then that we started to make some progress – we established that both his parents were very shy people. Miles remembered them always trying to avoid meeting new people. In fact, he even remembered a specific situation when they went on holiday when he was about 11. They were staying in a hotel on one of the Greek islands. It was the first evening and everyone was invited down to the bar for the introductory talk by the holiday representative. Miles actually remembered his parents talking about the meeting and deciding not to go because it would mean 'meeting new people for the first time'.

Miles thought he'd forgotten about this because it was such a long time ago – but he hadn't. Not only had he not forgotten about it, but he now realised it had had quite an impact on him and his own confidence levels. He'd started to be like his parents. He had no idea, of course, that this was happening – why should he? After all, he respected his parents and thought this was just normal behaviour.

Miles found that reflecting constructively on his upbringing really helped. In fact the holiday meeting was just one example of many that he started to remember. He could see that his own approach to life had been radically affected by the behaviour and approach of both his parents.

This was a major turning point for him. He had identified the source of his lack of confidence. He knew that he now had to break the habit and felt motivated to get on with it.

So, when reflecting back on your childhood, open your mind as much as you can. You're not only trying to think back to experiences and challenges you were faced with. You're also reflecting on relationships you had, the culture in which you were brought up and the way people close to you approached their own lives.

 **example**

Esther

Esther, a 42-year-old IT consultant, was beginning to feel that her life was being frittered away. She was happy in the sense that she was happily married and had two healthy teenage children. However, she was starting to feel that 'life was beginning to pass me by' and that she was missing out on opportunities. This was really starting to frustrate her. She put this down to her lack of self-confidence because she found it hard to take the first step towards doing anything new or different.

Like Miles in the previous example, she reflected on her life to see if she could identify anything that had happened to her that might explain this. She couldn't think of anything though. Then she started to think about how she had been brought up. She'd never really thought about the significance of this before. It turned out that her parents were very easygoing and, in her words, 'never encouraged me to meet new people, do exciting things or try to achieve anything more than being just average'.

The penny soon started to drop for Esther – she had grown into adulthood with the same approach. Like her parents, she couldn't help thinking that it was 'safer and more secure' to stay as you were rather than risk the dangers of trying new things. As a result, she'd always struggled to take a step into the unknown – she lacked the confidence to do this. She found it ▶

a huge relief to have found the answer and started to actively pursue new challenges in her life.

 **brilliant** tip

> Look further than just your experiences as an adult; think carefully about your childhood and the influences you came under.

It works the other way too:

 **brilliant** example

Ashley

Ashley couldn't work out why he never felt satisfied with his achievements. To his friends, 32-year-old Ashley was a successful web designer who had built up his own small company – he had his own company office with five people working for him. He was also a very talented sportsman.

He wasn't happy though. He knew this was something to do with his self-belief but couldn't quite put his finger on it. He thought back about his life and tried to work out if anything might have caused this. Like Miles and Esther though, he couldn't identify anything specific. Eventually he started to reflect on his upbringing.

He remembered that his father was 'incredibly ambitious' and that he had always expected Ashley to do well. He still remembered his father's favourite saying – 'Good isn't good enough Ashley ... excellent is where you need to be.'

Ashley was encouraged to play tennis from the age of five. He didn't mind this because he really enjoyed tennis. In fact, in his teens he played tennis for his county and won quite a few titles. However, even this success was never quite good enough for his father.

Eventually, Ashley started to lose his self-confidence and withdraw into himself. He couldn't reconcile why his father never seemed to be satisfied, even though Ashley thought he'd done well. Eventually he gave up tennis when he was 16.

As an adult, Ashley reflected and thought about how his father's approach had affected him. He began to realise that in fact he'd achieved a huge amount in his life so far. This simple exercise in looking back helped him to believe in himself, feel satisfied with his achievements and be more self-confident.

So what?

Miles, Esther and Ashley all learnt lessons by reflecting on how the attitudes of their parents had affected them in later life. It wasn't until they were encouraged to think about this that they realised the impact their childhood had had on them. Sometimes, we just accept certain behaviour to be normal when actually it is anything but. This is only to be expected when we haven't had an opportunity to experience behaviour that's any different – more often than not, this happens when we are young and protected by our parents from other influences.

But as we grow out of childhood, we become more aware of our surroundings. What people think of you starts to matter. You can't help but compare yourself to your peers. It starts to mean something to you when the realisation hits that you aren't as good at something as someone else. At this point, your self-belief can start to wane and, if you let it get the better of you, before you know it you're on the slippery slope to losing your self-confidence. What's worse, if someone criticises you, you take it to heart; if you fail at something, you feel embarrassed.

Realistically, we can't bring back that natural free spirit and enthusiasm that we used to have when we were young but we can certainly try to emulate it. Confident people can do this

confident people don't
let their concerns about
what other people think
affect them

– they don't let their concerns about what other people think affect them. This helps them to maintain the drive, enthusiasm and determination that we all used to have as children.

Keeping the balance

The three Brilliant Examples above reflect what could be described as 'negative attitudes'. Of course, when reflecting on your childhood, you will have remembered positive experiences and fun times too. Don't forget these – a tremendous amount can be learnt from those fun experiences you had as a child.

brilliant tip

Ask yourself how much your lack of self-belief and self-confidence may originate from your experiences and relationships when you were young.

Adulthood

So, you've reflected on your childhood. You've probably turned over a few stones that haven't been touched for a long time. You might have discovered something, just as Miles, Esther and Ashley did. Your discovery may well have been different to their experiences. Whatever it was, think positively about it and see it as a learning experience. Never let it be a weight around your neck.

On the other hand, it may be that you haven't discovered anything about your childhood that helps to explain your lack of self-confidence at this point in your life. Don't worry – all is not lost ...

Try thinking now about your life after you left home. What's happened since then?

Have you ever looked back and tried to identify actual events that happened or experiences you've had that may have had a knock-on effect on your confidence and self-belief? Well, this is definitely worth doing. Some people can remember a specific event that had a catastrophic impact on their confidence; others remember a series of smaller events that contributed; others can't really remember anything in particular but subconsciously know that past events have affected their confidence levels.

 **exercise**

Distant memories

Think back on your life. Think back as far as the time when you remember being more confident than you are now. If you think you've always lacked confidence, then reflect on the whole of your adult life.

Write down experiences you've had or events that have taken place that knocked your confidence levels and self-belief. If you can identify these, you've taken the first step to dealing with the negative impact they may have had. It never ceases to amaze me how important this exercise can be for some people. It's an exercise I encourage everyone who lacks self-confidence, self-belief or self-esteem to try.

Identify as much detail as you can about each memory:

● What happened?
● Why do you remember it?
● What can you learn from it?

Don't rush the exercise – you might not remember every experience straight away. Try mulling it over for a little while.

Some people come up with quite a comprehensive list of experiences; others only identify one major event. Try not to read on until you're happy you've had a good think about this.

Some of the following examples might help to jog your memory.

 **example**

Martha

Martha attended a confidence-building training course.

From the minute she arrived she was incredibly warm and friendly. In fact, to me she seemed very confident and for a while I wondered why she'd come. I almost asked her if she was in the right room! I noticed that she had a slight speech impediment and wondered if this might have something to do with the reason.

Everyone had a chance to introduce themselves. When it was Martha's turn she became very emotional. We were all astonished to hear that she felt her confidence had been completely blown away by just one very clear experience she'd had.

She'd been to a job interview six months before. She'd explained to the panel at the beginning of the interview that she used a hearing aid because she was partially deaf. This also meant that sometimes she didn't realise she was speaking louder than others and perhaps not quite as clearly.

She thought the interview had gone well because, at the end, two of the three people interviewing her gave her some very positive feedback and seemed happy. However, the third person on the panel (who happened to be the managing director) told Martha in a very direct and insensitive way that he thought she came across aggressively and therefore wouldn't fit in very well in their company. She was absolutely devastated – no one had ever described her as aggressive. She hated the thought of this because she prided herself in being a caring and sensitive person. All through her life she had worked in counselling-type roles and now she was being told she was aggressive – in her mind this meant she was totally unsuited to what she wanted to do.

Martha couldn't stop this experience affecting her mental attitude and approach to life. The more she thought about it, the more she lost her confidence until eventually, luckily, one of her friends suggested she needed to get some help.

During the training course she attended with us, she began to realise that it wasn't *her* that had the problem with aggression – it was the managing director. He had totally misread her. In his mind, she had come across as aggressive because she had to speak quite loudly because of her partial deafness. It was only during the training course that she started to realise that it was *his* behaviour that was wrong, not hers.

For the past six months Martha had focused on that one event – one person telling her one thing about herself. She'd completely forgotten that the other two people on the panel had told her she'd done really well. She'd also completely forgotten all the other successes she'd had in her counselling career and the positive things people had said about her. Martha had let this one negative event completely take over her life and blow her confidence away. It took a whole day (the duration of the course) for us to convince her that, in fact, it was the MD who had the problem, *not her*! He had completely misinterpreted her.

She walked away from the course as the person she used to be – looking forward to applying for interviews and to getting a new job.

---

brilliant tip

Try to get things in proportion. Don't let isolated events or experiences overpower your mindset. Confide in people who you know well and respect; explain to them the situation exactly as it happened and ask them how they interpret it. They may well see it differently to you. Then – very importantly – *believe* them.

You may have to think back quite a long way to pinpoint an experience that has affected your self-confidence. So keep an open mind here – don't make the assumption that only recent events are significant.

 **brilliant** example

Josh

I met Josh in November 2009. He was really struggling with his confidence levels. You wouldn't know this necessarily because he came across well when you met him and talked to him. He just seemed a little shy.

He was a big man physically and must have been in his mid-forties. He told me that he knew exactly when it was that he'd started to lose his confidence. It all revolved around a sporting injury he'd suffered.

He told me he used to play squash for England but that he had broken his foot and as a result he'd had to give up the sport completely. This had absolutely devastated him because his whole life revolved around squash. He had nothing to focus on any more, nothing to feel proud about and, what's more, he'd lost touch with his friends, almost all of whom came from the squash circuit.

I couldn't reconcile the fact that his physical build just didn't match that of a squash player. It was only when I asked him when the injury had happened that it started to make sense – I nearly fell off my chair when he said '14 May 1988'.

For 21 years, Josh had been letting his injury affect his self-belief and confidence. Only now could he see what an impact it had had on his life and how he needed to move on.

Both Josh and Martha had specific experiences they could identify. With the help of friends, they were able to move on. Try to identify the significance of experiences like these quickly so that you can come to terms with them. Otherwise you'll get stuck like Josh did. Martha was different; she managed to deal with the issue within months because she addressed it.

In short, when casting your mind back, consider these rules (and stick to them):

- Identify the experience.
- Accept it/come to terms with it.
- Learn from it.
- *Forget it.*

It could be that, having reflected, you remember a series of small events that has taken place and affected your confidence; there might not necessarily be one big event that overcomes everything else. That's fine – the principle remains the same. Don't dwell on the past for any longer than you need to.

> don't dwell on the past for any longer than you need to

Experiences you can learn from

Once you've identified it, don't forget the experience until you're sure you've learnt from it. Josh and Martha's experiences required them to change their mindset – there was nothing specific they could learn from them other than that, in future, they needed to be strong enough mentally not to let such experiences affect them.

You might not be able to remember a specific event like they did. Perhaps you've had a number of experiences, all of which have led to a dip or in your confidence or self-belief. If so, it might be helpful to list them – is there a theme to them? Do they tend to relate to your social life or your work life? Do they revolve around the same kind of situation? For example, some people find that every experience they've listed relates to a situation when they are socialising and meeting new people. Others find that the experiences are specifically to do with work, perhaps attending meetings or giving presentations.

Regardless of what you come up with and uncover, the same rules apply. Having identified and come to terms with the experiences (and possibly a theme), now ask yourself what you can learn from them. What went wrong? What went right? In asking yourself these questions, you're looking for the answers to these two questions:

- Would it be worth trying to pre-empt and prepare better for the situation next time?
- What might I benefit from doing differently next time?

Finding the answers to these two questions will set you well on the way to building your self-confidence. We'll come back to this theme later when we deal with preparation.

Accepting your personal challenge

The fact that you're reading *Brilliant Self Confidence* suggests you've already decided you need to boost your confidence levels. It's great that you've taken the first major step on the road. Some people get stuck in a groove and don't manage to get this far.

There are two questions you should ask yourself at this point:

- Do you *really* want to change?
- Are you prepared to accept that you'll need to do some things differently from now on?

Be honest with yourself when you answer these questions. They could be the difference between success and failure.

You might be slightly unsure, particularly with regard to the second question – after all you don't yet know what the change involves. Don't worry about that for the moment – right now it's just important you realise that feeling and coming across as more confident will definitely mean doing some things differently. You'll need to accept that this might be difficult. You'll probably have to break some

you'll probably have to break *some* habits, possibly habits of a lifetime habits, possibly habits of a lifetime. No one ever finds this easy.

But don't get the wrong idea here. Don't start getting depressed! These comments are designed to prepare you for the challenge ahead. 'Challenge' is a very appropriate word for this. You should see your endeavours to build your confidence as exactly that – a challenge.

Try to think of your journey to greater confidence as a personal project: your 'Self-Confidence Project'. As with all projects it will only succeed if it is planned and prepared for thoroughly. The project needs to have a clear objective which is measurable – i.e. 'to achieve something by a certain date'. It helps to start thinking like this. For example – your strategic, long-term objective is to build your self-confidence. You've probably already worked that out. But have you thought about how that new self-confidence is going to show itself? Have you thought about what you're going to do with it once you have it? If you haven't, you're missing a trick.

After all, it would be daft to pass your driving test with flying colours and then get in your car with no idea of where you're going!

You'll need to break down your strategic objective into smaller chunks. Each of these chunks will have its own more tactical goals. *Brilliant Self Confidence* is written in a logical way. You'll be able to set your tactical goals as you progress through the text. Accepting your personal challenge becomes a lot easier if you take small steps at a time.

So, if you approach your Self-Confidence Project on an incremental basis, the whole challenge will feel more manageable. Try approaching each chapter as shown in Figure 1.1.

This process will really help you to achieve your ultimate objective. Once you get the hang of it, you'll see how helpful the process is. *It makes you act*, rather than just read the book.

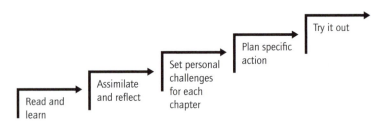

Figure 1.1 Approaching your Self-Confidence Project: a road map

Starting your Self-Confidence Project

To get started, think about the situations where your lack of confidence lets you down. You're trying to identify situations in which you feel most out of your comfort zone. These could be 'everyday' situations or they could be more significant specific events. They could have happened as a 'one-off' or they could be experiences that you have regularly. Cover both your personal life and your work life. Try to keep the two separate because you might decide to deal with them differently. The first step to dealing with a problem is to identify the issue.

 **brilliant** exercise

Stumbling blocks

You'll need to write down and record each situation or event you find difficult so that it becomes a focus for you. As you move on through *Brilliant Self Confidence*, these stumbling blocks are going to form a major part of your Self-Confidence Project.

Try to include as much detail as possible – break each situation or event down and try to cover the following:

● Describe the situation or event. (Example – networking events at work.)
● Describe why you find these difficult. (Example – because I don't know anyone and find it difficult to talk to people I haven't met before.)

- Describe what you think you do physically to show your lack of confidence. (Example - try to avoid people, let other people talk, feel uncomfortable with silences, look nervous, fidget, waffle.)
- Describe how you feel inside. (Example - pathetic, embarrassed, insecure, uptight, frustrated.)

---

brilliant tip

The first step to dealing with a problem is to identify it.

Now look to the future.

Think about how you would like to feel when you find yourself in the same situation again. Be positive and ambitious here – have some belief in yourself.

Write your thoughts down. Don't read on until you've finished.

Perhaps you've come up with something like this: 'When I go to my next networking meeting, I would like to feel confident, in control, relaxed, at ease and I would like to enjoy myself.'

Great! You're now thinking positively. To succeed with the *Brilliant Self Confidence* ethic, you must start as you mean to go on. It's absolutely true that if you don't aspire to something, you won't have a focus; if you don't have a focus, you'll never achieve it.

> if you don't aspire to something, you won't have a focus; if you don't have a focus, you'll *never* achieve it

brilliant tip

What you visualise, you believe and what you practise, you become.

Now you're all set up. You know the situations that are troubling you and you have a vision of how you'd like to feel in the future. There's just one more thing that you'll need to come to terms with before we move on: *your mind* – is it working for you or against you?

brilliant recap

Chapter 1

- No one is born confident; confidence is a skill you can learn.

- Overcoming self-doubt is one of the keys to feeling more confident.

- You don't have to be talented, good-looking or clever to be confident.

- Try to approach challenges with an open mind as you did when you were young.

- Identify the situations where you lack confidence most, accept them as part of life, learn from these experiences, think about how you will approach them next time and then forget them.

- Look to the future with a positive mindset. A problem is a challenge to be solved, not a nightmare to be avoided.

Being and feeling more positive

Having a positive mental attitude

'It is not the mountain we conquer but ourselves.'

Sir Edmund Hillary, mountaineer and explorer

Doubters beware!

Before you continue here, it's important that you open your mind to what you are going to read.

It might help if I let you into a secret. I used to be a person who didn't believe in positive thinking. I used to think that people who talked about thinking positively were just kidding themselves. I was convinced they were just playing mind games with themselves.

I remember thinking that surely they must be confused if they really believed that the simple act of just *thinking positively* would help them.

How wrong I was.

In fact, it wasn't until I started studying the subject and trying out some of the concepts for myself that I realised. I regret not keeping an open mind.

There's no doubt that not everyone accepts or believes in positive thinking. So, if you're a doubter, bear with me here – remember, I too was a sceptic once. Accepting that positive thinking works is the first step: only then can you start to consider how to achieve it and then how to use it effectively to build your confidence.

And don't forget – it's absolutely true that optimistic people are more likely to stay healthy and live longer than pessimists!

We know this because researchers at the University of Pittsburgh studied data from the Women's Health Initiative, an ongoing study of 100,000 women over 50 that started in 1994. At the beginning of the study, participants were asked to respond to whether they agreed with a statement like 'In uncertain times, I expect the worst'. Eight years later, researchers examined the women's death rates and found that those who were optimistic were 14 per cent more likely to be alive than the pessimists.

Where do you stand?

'The optimist sees the doughnut, the pessimist sees the hole.'

Oscar Wilde

How do you describe yourself when someone asks you if you are a positive or a negative thinker? If you're not sure, it's important to be clear on this before moving on.

Try asking yourself if you see your glass as half full or half empty. If it's half full, you're thinking the right way; you're likely to think more positively. If more often than not you see it as half empty, then you need to start trying to change your mindset straight away.

Consider also how you perceive events in your life. If you're feeling down or frustrated because you pay a lot of tax, the positive in this is that you probably earn a lot of money. If someone tells you you look tired or unwell, the positive in this is that they care about you. So, how hard do you find it to see these positives?

If you're still not sure where you stand here, try looking back over the last year – ask yourself what you remember. You'll probably have a mixture of good and bad memories. The key here is to establish which ones are taking precedence. Where does your focus tend to be? If you're thinking mainly of good experiences, well done – you're thinking positively. If you're thinking mainly of negatives, you need to start thinking about trying to shift your mindset.

We've already established (during Chapter 1) that negative memories have value if you can learn from them. Once that's happened and you've squeezed out everything you can learn from them, you must forget them and move on. Confident people have the self-discipline to do this. They understand the dangers of constantly thinking back to negative experiences. They won't let these negative memories overpower the positive times. In essence, confident people think *positively* all the time.

> confident people have the mental discipline to think *positively* all the time

Mind over matter?

Anne Frank suffered unimaginable pressures while hiding in a secret annexe in Amsterdam during World War II. This quote from her diary gives some clues as to how she remained positive.

'I don't think of all the misery but of the beauty that still remains.'

Anne Frank, *The Diary of a Young Girl*

Positive thinking is a state of mind. It's a mental attitude that helps to steer your mind towards thoughts and actions that are conducive to self-belief and confidence. People who demonstrate a strong mental attitude and positive mindset anticipate and look forward to fulfilment and happiness. Their self-belief and positive attitude anticipate and expect success, not failure.

Just as we have our own physical habits, so we have mental habits. The difficulty is that physical habits are more obvious; you can see them and address them if necessary. Mental habits are more of a challenge; they're hidden and often only *you* know what they are. So addressing a bad mental habit requires real determination, particularly if it relates to negative thinking.

Who do you know who you would describe as a positive thinker? I'll bet you would also describe this person as having self-belief and self-confidence. That's because the two go together. The majority of confident people think positively.

So how do they manage to do this? Confident people do a number of things that help them to stay positive in their attitude. You'll see as we move on that these things aren't complicated. In fact they're very simple and sometimes quite subtle. You should be able to try them out yourself straight away. But manage your expectations and be realistic. Don't get too carried away – attitude and thoughts take time to change. It's not going to happen overnight.

brilliant tip

People who lean towards negative thinking tend to forget the good things they do or that happen to them. You should remind yourself of these regularly, otherwise they'll get lost in a cloud of negativity.

Do you doubt yourself?

'A man is but the product of his thoughts; what he thinks, he becomes.'

Mahatma Gandhi

You'd be superhuman if you didn't doubt yourself on occasions. Confident people doubt themselves too but they've learnt how to control this. They won't let self-doubt hold them back.

From self-doubt comes procrastination: that unseen and negative influence which leads you to put things off – sometimes things that really matter. We normally know when this has happened but, more often than not, it's too late by then. The damage has been done; that opportunity you should have seized has gone.

Have you ever tried to work out why you sometimes doubt yourself? Quite often it's because someone else sows that seed of doubt. But why listen to someone who talks negatively about you unless they've got something constructive to say? Think about it … there's absolutely no point because there's nothing helpful to be gained.

Michael Caine worked this out early in his life when his headmaster told him, 'You will be a labourer all your life.' *He didn't let this stop him.*

Walt Disney worked it out too. He was fired by a newspaper editor because 'he lacked imagination and had no good ideas'. He went bankrupt several times before he built Disneyland. In fact, the proposed park was rejected by the city of Anaheim on the grounds that it would only attract riffraff. *He didn't let it stop him.*

And Harrison Ford is a good example too. After his first acting performance as a hotel bellhop in the film *Dead Heat on a Merry-Go-Round,* the studio vice-president called him into his office. 'Sit down kid,' the studio head said, 'I want to tell you a story … The first time Tony Curtis was ever in a movie he delivered a bag of groceries. We took one look at him and knew he was a movie star.' Ford replied, 'I thought you were supposed to think that he was a grocery delivery boy.' The vice-president dismissed Ford with 'You ain't got it kid, you ain't got it … now get out of here.' *Harrison Ford didn't let it stop him either.*

Don't take it personally

Try not to take failure personally; easy to say but not so easy to do. Look around you. You're not the only one who fails on occasions. After his first audition, Sidney Poitier was told by the casting director, 'Why don't you stop wasting people's time and go out and become a dishwasher or something?' It was at that moment, recalls Poitier, that he decided to devote his life to acting.

Self-doubt can also show itself because 'society' sees failure as bad. You're seen to be weak and inadequate if you fail. So, not surprisingly, we fear failure. But how can you deal with that fear? It might never go away completely but there are ways of controlling it.

One thing's certain; if you don't do *something*, you'll never overcome self-doubt. So try this simple process:

Take action

'Only those who dare to fail greatly can achieve greatly.'

Robert F. Kennedy.

The best way to reduce fear and build self-confidence is to take action. One way to spur yourself on is to remember that playing safe (doing nothing) has risks too. Others could be acting and changing for the better around you. So you may well get left behind. So consider the cost; others could be seizing the opportunities you could have had.

Prepare yourself though. The first time you do something new is always the hardest. Think of jumping from the highest board

Figure 2.1 Taking action

into the swimming pool, skiing down a steep run, standing up to do your first formal presentation, chairing your first meeting, or perhaps just contributing for the first time during a meeting. Whatever it is, the first time you do it is the most challenging.

Persist

'Our greatest glory is not in never falling but in rising every time we fall.'

Confucius

Life is life. Things don't always work out the way you plan them. But you don't need me to tell you that. Confident people accept this when it happens and persist. If it doesn't work first time, they try again, perhaps with a slightly different approach. So, if someone doesn't listen to you the first time, don't give up. There's a reason why the first attempt didn't work so try a different approach the second time. Have a contingency plan – have a 'Plan B' in place; you might even need a 'Plan C'.

After Fred Astaire's first screen test, the memo from the testing director of MGM, dated 1933, read, 'Can't act. Can't sing. Slightly bald. Can dance a little.' He kept that memo over the fireplace in his Beverly Hills home. Astaire once observed that 'when you're experimenting, you have to try so many things before you choose what you want, that you may go days getting nothing but exhaustion.' And here is the reward for perseverance: 'The higher up you go, the more mistakes you're allowed. Right at the top, if you make enough of them, it's considered to be your style.'

Learn from the experience

A failure to one person is a learning experience to another, and that's the secret.

Thomas Edison's teachers said he was 'too stupid to learn anything'. He was fired from his first two jobs for being 'non-productive'. As an inventor, Edison made 1,000 unsuc-cessful attempts at inventing the light bulb. When a reporter asked, 'How did it feel to fail 1,000 times?' Edison replied, 'I didn't fail 1,000 times. The light bulb was an invention with 1,000 steps.'

Winston Churchill failed academically at school. He was sub-sequently defeated in every election for public office until he became Prime Minister at the age of 62. He later wrote, 'Never give in, never give in, never, never, never, never – in nothing, great or small, large or petty – never give in except to convictions of honour and good sense. Never, Never, Never, Never give up.'

And Thomas Watson, Sr, founder of IBM, put his finger on it when he said, '*If you want to increase your success rate, double your failure rate.*'

A few other tips to help overcome self-doubt

Burn the boats – When ancient Greek armies travelled across the sea to do battle, the first thing they would do after landing was to burn the boats, leaving them stranded. With no way to make it home besides victory, the resolve of the soldiers was strength-ened. When success and failure are the only options, you have no choice but to follow through.

Think of the worst case scenario – Get things in perspective by con-sidering the worst that can happen if you fail. Sometimes (but very rarely) the worst case scenario may be genuinely disastrous, and it may be perfectly rational to fear failure. In most cases, though, this worst case scenario may not actually be that bad. Recognising and accepting this can really help.

Manage your expectations – Don't bite off more than you can chew. Tread carefully initially when trying something new. No one is perfect, so expect to fail on occasions. If you manage your expecta-tions, when you fail, you'll fall from a height you can recover from.

So how can you start to help yourself to become more optimistic and to think more positively?

 **exercise**

Homework

Each night before you go to bed, try writing down three positive things that happened or that you did during the day. Sounds bonkers, doesn't it! But try it. It really will help you to keep these positive things in the forefront of your mind. Do this every night for the foreseeable future.

Some people find it helpful to buy a small notebook for this. This will make it easier to keep the list together and to reflect on the positives you record. It won't be long before you have a comprehensive list. Use this list to remind yourself regularly of the positives in your life. This is one small exercise that will help to keep you thinking positively.

Eliminate negative thoughts

When you think back and reflect on your memories, which ones do you think of first: the good times or the bad times? This can often be a good indicator of whether you're a positive or negative thinker.

Come to terms with where you stand here. If you tend to think negatively, don't let it happen; it's destructive. When a negative thought comes into your mind, be aware of it, then try to replace it with a positive, constructive one. The negative thought probably won't go away easily, so persevere each time it enters your mind; make sure you replace it with a positive one every time it happens. Eventually your mind will learn how to think positively and ignore negative thoughts.

Try to do this even when your life isn't going as you would like it to or when you're worried about something. This will be the hardest time to think positively because negative thoughts will be most prominent. Train your mind to expect only positive results – believe that, at some point, your life will change for the better. You can speed up this process if you really want to.

brilliant tip

Write it down every time a negative thought comes into your mind. Sometimes you don't realise how much you're doing it until you actually see it in black and white.

Don't forget that positive and negative thinking are contagious. A negative attitude can show itself in your body language. This tends to happen on a subconscious level but can still have a signif-

positive and negative thinking are contagious

icant impact on others. For example, socially, people don't tend to want to be around negative thinkers because they find them depressing; they find positive people more exciting and interesting. So, negative thinking can have an impact on your friendships and ultimately on your social life too.

Your work life can also be dramatically affected: negative people aren't seen as people with potential and therefore are less likely to be promoted. Just think about it – how many successful business people do you know who think negatively? The answer must surely be none.

brilliant tip

Stop negative thinking. If you think you're going to fail, you'll feel like a failure; if you feel like a failure, you will fail.

Stop negative language

Of course, if you think more positively, the likelihood is that your message will be more positive when you speak it – that should come naturally. Watch out though, because you could have a habit of saying things that aren't helping you.

 **example**

Costas

Costas was working for a merchant bank and had gone through their graduate training scheme. He was now in his third year as a full-time employee.

He'd recently had a performance appraisal and his manager had told him he thought he lacked self-confidence. His manager said he 'couldn't put his finger on it' but there was something about Costas that he felt portrayed a lack of confidence.

Costas agreed with him because he too felt his confidence could be boosted and they decided to book him on to a confidence-building training course. So, Costas arrived on the course and within 30 seconds he started saying something that portrayed him as a person who lacked confidence. He was a serial 'sorry sayer'. He would apologise for everything. First he apologised for being late, even though he was in fact five minutes early – he just felt that he was letting the others down because they had arrived earlier than him. Then he apologised for sitting down because he wondered if someone else would prefer his seat. Then he said sorry for introducing himself because he wondered if anyone else might like to talk before he did. He would then apologise every time he wanted to ask a question. Almost everything he said was prefixed by the word 'sorry'.

The start of the course was about discovering why you lack confidence and why others perceive you as lacking confidence. When Costas was told, he was surprised to hear that he said sorry a lot. He really didn't have any idea!

We told him each time he said sorry as the day went on. Most of the time, he wasn't even aware that he'd done it – it had become such a habit for him. He found this to be a massive learning experience. I'd been making notes and by the end of the day he'd said sorry 59 times! Not one of those times was necessary.

You might not think it but what you say does have an impact on how positive (or negative) you actually feel. Some people really struggle to come to terms with this. Confident people speak positive language. This helps them to stay positive in their mental attitude.

Saying sorry when an apology isn't appropriate sends negative signals to your mind. It also communicates a submissive message to the other person. It isn't a positive and confident action and therefore isn't conducive to developing self-belief and self-confidence. If taken to an extreme it can also lead to feelings of insecurity and inferiority.

brilliant tip

Don't say sorry unless it would be impolite not to or unless you've actually hurt or offended someone. Confident people are polite but only say sorry when an apology is warranted.

Here's a question for you: when someone asks you a question like 'How are you?' or 'How are things going?' what do you say in reply? Think carefully about this because you probably have a standard reply regardless of how you're actually feeling. People who don't make a conscious effort to think positively tend to reply to this question in a negative way. They'll say 'Not bad, thanks' or 'OK, thanks' in an unenthusiastic way. You're not going to sound and feel confident and positive when you reply like this (try saying it now to yourself and you'll see what I mean). If you have a negative mindset, a reply like this becomes your normal reply, even when you're having a *good* day! Why on earth would you want to give the impression things are only going 'OK' or things 'aren't too bad' when actually things are good? That's just silly.

So, how about being more positive the next time someone greets you and asks how things are going. Try saying 'Good, thanks' or, if you really want to push the boat out, 'Really good, thanks'. You'll be amazed at how much more positive you start to feel simply by speaking positive language. This really does work – you'll have to try it to see.

Of course, not only do you feel more positive – the person you're talking to sees you as a positive person and will subconsciously register this. The person is much more likely to want to help you, work with you, socialise with you, listen to you ... and the list goes on.

brilliant tip

Start practising your new reply when someone asks you how you are. Keep practising because breaking an old habit is never easy. Watch the person's face carefully – you'll see a more positive reaction from now on! This is bound to help you to stay positive yourself.

You might have read these points about negative language and thought they are not relevant to you. You wouldn't be the first person to do this. A word of warning here: *be careful* ... don't presume you don't think negatively because sometimes people just can't see or hear it in themselves. Costas was a perfect example.

Apologising unnecessarily is just one example of negative language. There are others too ...

 **example**

Julie

Julie was conscious that she seemed to be bumbling through life. Although she enjoyed her job as a post lady, she was getting bored. Furthermore, her life had been turned upside down about six months earlier because, out of the blue, her husband told her he was leaving her after 12 years of marriage. This had really knocked her back.

Julie got more and more depressed and became very introverted although, in fact, she was quite a bubbly and extroverted person normally. When she explained her predicament and talked generally about her situation she couldn't see that her language was overwhelmingly negative. She had a habit of saying particular words and phrases that had a negative connotation. For example, one of her favourite phrases was 'if only'.

She had no idea that this was handicapping any possibility of her achieving a positive mindset. Her whole demeanour, even her body language, exuded this negativity.

The most frustrating thing for Julie was that she knew what she wanted to do with her life. Her plan was already in her mind. She wanted more independence – she wanted to be her own boss. She loved interior design and wanted to buy and sell property. She had some capital from the divorce and a property sale. With no children and no other responsibilities, she knew in her heart of hearts that, really, there should be nothing stopping her buying her first property.

The problem was that she was continually putting barriers up for herself because of her negative language. She just couldn't see what effect this was having on her mental attitude and mood – she needed other people to tell her.

Unless someone knows you very well (and even then it's doubtful), people aren't just going to volunteer information.

Understandably, they'll worry about hurting your feelings or appearing rude. So, the best way to get someone to give you some feedback is to invite them.

 **exercise**

Talk the talk

Try asking a good friend or relation to help you here. Ask them to tell you every time you say something negative. You might get a surprise! Give them some feedback on their language as well of course – they might learn something they didn't know too.

Once you know if you have a habit of saying something in particular, make a conscious effort to listen to yourself while you're speaking. This should help you to kick the habit.

Worriers

We all worry on occasions – it's only natural. However, some people are able to control their worries and not let them interfere with their lives to any great extent. It's true that some people are more 'easygoing' than others but even they worry sometimes. Unfortunately, if you're a 'natural worrier', you'll have to work harder on this than they might.

Controlling the effect that worrying has on your mental attitude is a vital component of maintaining a positive mindset. The simple way to do this is to have the self-discipline to keep your worries *in proportion*.

> have the self-discipline to keep your worries *in proportion*

Natural worriers always have to have something to worry about. If there's nothing major to worry about in their life at the time, they'll worry about something small.

 **example**

Christian

Christian told us this story during a confidence-building session.

He'd been staying with friends and was preparing for a long drive home. He got up early and packed his bag ready to go. He filled a flask with coffee, grabbed his bag and got into the car.

Half an hour later he was driving along and realised he'd forgotten his flask. It was too late to turn back because he had to catch a ferry which otherwise he would miss. Christian was a natural worrier – he just couldn't get the flask out of his mind. It wasn't just the fact that he'd forgotten it and wouldn't be able to drink the coffee in it. He couldn't help worrying about all the other implications of leaving the flask. He worried about not having it for his fishing trip next weekend; he worried about not having it for his son's rugby match on Wednesday; he worried that he wouldn't have it if he broke down … and in fact, that's exactly what happened – he did break down. Of course, at that point, he completely forgot about his flask. He had something else to worry about now – something probably worthy of a little bit of worry.

It was an interesting lesson for him – once he'd reflected on it he could see how out of proportion his worrying was.

brilliant tip

Try to get your worries in perspective. Think about the worst thing that could possibly happen, then scale down and down again. Think about what's worrying you right at this very moment while you're reading this. Is it really that bad? Confident people get their worries in proportion.

 **recap**

Chapter 2

- Don't underestimate the power of positive thinking. If you're a cynic, keep an open mind.

- Come to terms with where you stand – are you an optimist or a pessimist? This could mean changing your mindset.

- It's natural to doubt yourself, even 'confident' people do.

- It's essential to have the courage to take action. Doing something and failing is better than doing nothing at all: Act, Persist, Learn.

- Eliminate negative thoughts and cut out negative language.

- We all worry on occasions, but try to get your worries in proportion.

Knowing what you want to achieve

Setting positive objectives and goals

'Begin with the end in mind.'

Stephen Covey, author and management consultant

To feel confident, you need to be focused; focus brings satisfaction and a sense that you're not wasting your time.

Do you ever think seriously about what you want to achieve during your lifetime? Do you ever reflect and ask yourself if you're *making the most* of your life? Or are you like the majority of people – going from day to day, busily doing the things that need to be done but never really thinking seriously about why you're doing them?

People who make the most of their lives have a sense of purpose about them. They know why they do things. How do they know this? In short, because they're *focused* and they have a plan. They know what they want to achieve and they've worked out how to achieve it.

This is essential to keeping a positive mindset and feeling more confident.

> people who make the most of their lives have a sense of purpose about them

Try thinking about it like this – you've got two options open to you, a choice of two paths to take ...

Option 1 – Carry on as normal, have no focus, drift, achieve nothing, feel even less confident … and ultimately, fall into the bottomless pit of no self-confidence.

Figure 3.1 Bottomless pit

Option 2 – Have the courage to have a go. Be ready for a tough climb, though. Be prepared to fail, learn from the failure, decide on another plan, act, succeed, feel more confident. Think like this and you will reach the summit of confidence mountain.

Figure 3.2 Confidence mountain

Unfortunately there are no prizes for guessing the right option! So how do you get Option 2 moving?

You could start by asking yourself:

- What were you doing five years ago?
- What's happened since then?
- But more significantly – What have you *achieved* since then?

These questions should get you thinking about whether or not you're making the most of your life. Be straight and honest with yourself. Don't try to find excuses. If you haven't achieved a great deal, then acknowledge that and accept it. Don't blame yourself, there's no point. Your job now is to make a commitment to not letting the same happen over the next five years.

If they're honest, most people do come to the conclusion that they haven't achieved as much as they could or should have. This is valuable information – but it's meaningless if you don't treat it as a lesson. If it's a lesson, you can learn from it – and that's exactly what you're going to do.

Here's how …

Positive thinkers focus on the future – and that's what you *must* start doing if you want to build your self-belief and self-confidence. Other than learning from your mistakes and realising you haven't achieved what you could have, looking back isn't going to help you *now*. That time has gone.

So the next part of your Self-Confidence Project involves taking a big step forward. Actually, a better description would be a *huge leap* forward. That's why I've called it the Cornerstone. You're going to pick up this stone, set it firmly and build your confidence on it.

 **brilliant** exercise

Cornerstone

This 'Cornerstone' exercise is going to form a major part of your Self-Confidence Project. Be prepared to take some time over it. It's important not to rush it. If you commit to it fully, it will achieve exactly what its name suggests – it will act as the strong cornerstone upon which your Project is built. The exercise involves a number of steps. Stop after each step to reflect – you might decide to change something on reflection.

Step 1 – Strategic thinking

Try projecting your thoughts into the future. You're looking between two and five years ahead. In other words, you're looking strategically at your life over a period of time. I find that younger people, say in their twenties or early thirties, sometimes prefer to look two or three years ahead – five years can seem like a long time at this age. So choose a period of time that suits *you*. Remember, you're thinking strategically so it shouldn't be any less than two years.

It's important to differentiate between your work life and your personal life. We've already touched on the importance of achieving a balance to your life if you want to feel more confident and positive. Differentiating between work and personal life will help with this.

Now start to open your mind and think about what you'd like to achieve over this strategic period of time. Your ultimate aim here is to set some strategic objectives and bring some direction and focus to your life.

Let's just take a couple of minutes to reflect here. I'm trying to picture what you're up to – in other words; what's going on in your mind as you read this and how you're getting on. I've asked you to think about what you want to achieve over the next few years. If you're like a lot of people I meet, you could well be sitting there staring at a blank piece of paper. Don't worry! This can be a challenging task to start, but once you get going you'll find it easier. If you need it, I have a plan to help you get moving.

On the other hand, if you've started already and your 'strategic' picture is forming, keep going. Still, the following idea might help. Make sure you're feeling fresh and you're in a positive mood when you start this exercise.

 **exercise**

Mind maps

You'll need a blank piece of A4 paper and a pen. You're going to use them to create a 'mind map'. Mind mapping is a simple and very practical creative thinking process. It involves jotting down everything you can think of that has relevance to the strategic period you are looking ahead at in your life; consider your needs, your wants, your aspirations, your responsibilities, your family, your career – and anything else you think is important.

Mind maps only work if you challenge yourself to be bold and imaginative. Don't be scared to write down your aspirations. This will help you to think creatively.

 **example**

Emma

28-year-old Emma lived in Central London with her partner, Matt. She had a three-year-old daughter, Millie, and had plans to get married. She worked part time, as did Matt. They took turns during the week to look after Millie.

Emma completed the Cornerstone exercise. She started by developing the following mind map. It gives you a good feel for the concept of mind mapping. You'll see she's covered all aspects of her life.

▶

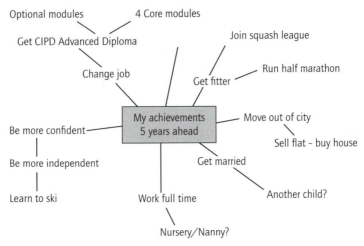

Figure 3.3 Emma's mind map

Don't move on with the Cornerstone exercise until you've produced a mind map that you're happy with. Have a shot at it and then leave it for a day or so. Don't rush it. Reflect on it. Some people like to share their thoughts with their partner or a close relation. There's nothing wrong with this but be careful that person doesn't influence you, dampen your enthusiasm or put you off in any way. It's your strategic plan, not theirs.

Do whatever you need to do to create a mind map that paints a strategic picture for you.

Step 2 – Strategic objectives

 **brilliant** definition

The strategic objectives you create here will form the platform upon which the next stage of your life is built. They're one of the key elements of your Self-Confidence Project.

Once you have your mind map, the next step is to use it to form strategic objectives. At the moment you've got a piece of paper with ideas scribbled all over it. Developing strategic objectives from it converts the mind map into something meaningful. Think carefully about this – you're going to use these objectives to drive what you do for the foreseeable future.

It's important that you're realistic during this exercise. For each objective you set, you're striving for the balance between challenge and achievability. Yes, you should challenge yourself but don't be so ambitious that deep down you know you won't be able to achieve your objectives. If just one objective loses credibility, your enthusiasm to achieve the others is likely to wane.

Each time you decide on and commit to an objective, ask yourself if you'll be able to assess whether or not you've achieved it. You won't be able to do this if the objective isn't specific or if it's not measurable in some way. Don't forget the time aspect either. Yes, these are strategic objectives but that doesn't necessarily mean that every one of them is to be achieved over the five-year period. It may make sense to aim to achieve some of them over the shorter term. For this exercise, the shorter term shouldn't be less than two years though.

Use this simple mnemonic to keep you on track when you're setting objectives. Consider each word in the mnemonic and reconcile the objective against it.

Specific – Is it specific enough? Will you know what it means when you try to assess whether or not you've achieved it?

Measurable – How will you assess whether or not it has actually been achieved? What measures will you use?

Achievable – You're looking for the balance between achievability and challenge. Have you thought seriously about the resources you'll need? Does it stand up in terms of time required, money, support, etc.

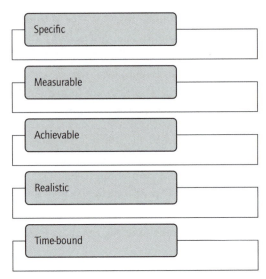

Figure 3.4 Goal setting

Realistic – Are you kidding yourself? Is it just a dream? Or does it make sense and is it really going to help you to achieve more?

Time-bound – Have you set a date to achieve it by? If not, it will drift on and, potentially, fizzle out.

Here are *just some* of the strategic objectives Emma developed from her mind map. They give you a feel for the transition you need to make between mind map and objective setting.

You can see that Emma's strategic objectives are specific, measurable and timebound. They're also strategic in the sense that they project years ahead, not months ahead. While she was setting them she also thought carefully about whether she felt they were achievable and realistic. In essence, her objectives are SMART. They stand up to all five of the SMART criteria.

She'll know whether or not she's achieved each one because she can assess it. She hasn't finished yet though. She needs to start thinking shorter term or more 'tactically' now – she needs to

Emma's strategic objectives – two to five years ahead

Career/Work life	Personal life
To be working full time by December 2014	To sell flat and buy two-bedroom house out of city by December 2014
To study for and achieve a CIPD Advanced Diploma in HR Management by December 2015	To run a half marathon by December 2014
To get a job in HR management by September 2016	To get married by August 2015
	To ski a black (difficult) ski run by April 2015

focus on each objective in its own right and consider what needs to happen to get it moving.

Step 3 – Tactical thinking

This helps you to set out what you need to do in the shorter term to gets things moving. Tactical thinking bridges the gap between the present and the strategic, longer term. Let's take one or two of Emma's strategic objectives, one personal and one work related and use them to show how tactical thinking works.

One of her strategic objectives in her work life is 'to study for and achieve a CIPD Advanced Diploma in HR Management by December 2015'.

Tactical goals

She's now thinking more tactically – so she's looking at the next six months. Each strategic objective has to be supported by tactical goals. Therefore, to support her CIPD Diploma objective, she decided to set herself the following goals to be achieved over the next six months. She's already researched the cost of attending a course and she's happy that she can afford it:

Goal 1: To research institutions which run part-time/home-study CIPD Diplomas in Management and decide on the best course by end of month 1.

Goal 2: To send applications to at least four Institutions by the end of month 2.

Goal 3: To start the CIPD Diploma by the end of 2013.

One of Emma's objectives in her personal life is 'To run a half marathon by December 2014'. She's given herself two years to achieve this because, at the present time, she sees herself as generally unfit and doesn't do any running at all.

Again, Emma needs to look at this objective in a shorter term, more day-to-day context. So she's decided to set herself the following more tactical objectives over the next six months.

- To be able to jog 2 miles and to swim 10 lengths by the end of month 1.
- To be able to jog 3 miles and to swim 15 lengths by the end of month 2.
- To be able to jog 4 miles and to swim 20 lengths by the end of month 3.
- To be able to jog 5 miles and to swim 25 lengths by the end of month 4.
- To be able to jog 6 miles and to swim 30 lengths by the end of month 5.
- To be able to jog 7 miles and to swim 35 lengths by the end of month 6.

To some this might seem like a very 'regimented' approach. Well that's exactly what it is. And that's exactly how you'll need to approach your own tactical goals. There's no 'wishy washyness' – Emma knows exactly what she needs to do. You'll find that being crystal clear about your tactical goals helps you to feel more motivated to achieve them.

Step 4 – Personal action plan

Now that your tactical goals are clear, you need to put together a plan of action. This details what you have to do on a weekly basis in order to achieve these tactical goals.

Following these four logical steps – mind map, strategic objectives, tactical goals, action plan – helps you to feel more in control of your life. It disciplines you to break down your strategic plans into manageable chunks that actually feel achievable and believable.

Emma took it step by step. She concentrated on one month at a time – initially, she focused on the first week of month 1. For example, with her fitness tactical goals she decided that to achieve the one-month goal, she would need to jog one mile twice and swim five lengths twice during the first week. She lived about a mile away from the swimming pool so she would jog there and back when she went.

With her CIPD goals, she decided that to achieve Goal 1, she'd need to spend one evening each week for the next three weeks researching courses. She'd do this on Wednesday evening because she had no other commitments planned.

brilliant tip

Help yourself to keep a positive mental attitude by looking into the future and challenging yourself by setting meaningful objectives.

Don't forget ... objective setting should be a continuous process. Life is life; things change. It may well be that something completely unforeseen happens that you could never have predicted when you set your strategic objectives. Don't make the mistake of blaming yourself but also, don't use it as an excuse to give up. Simply reflect on what it means for the objective and reset it. You're better off having a plan that changes than no plan at all ...

You should regularly review your plans, take account of any unforeseen eventualities, make amendments where necessary and set new objectives and goals when others have been achieved.

Remember the sequence charted in Figure 3.5; it will stand you in good stead and provide you with a solid platform from which to work.

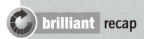 **brilliant** recap

Chapter 3

- Knowing what you want to achieve is essential to confident behaviour.
- Be focused and have the self-discipline to set yourself challenges.
- Force yourself to look to the future.
- Learn from the past but don't dwell on it, just move on.
- Use a mind map to creatively identify your aspirations at work, socially and at home.
- Feel more motivated by setting meaningful personal goals which really help you to achieve more.

Figure 3.5 Personal planning sequence

PART 2

Communicating with self-confidence

How do people see you?

'It is good to see ourselves as others see us.'

Mahatma Gandhi

Have you ever thought about how people perceive you? I mean *seriously* thought about it? It's true that we all wonder what people think of us every now and then. But it's also true that we tend to wonder this through curiosity rather than for any constructive reason.

Getting to the bottom of how people perceive you is one of the essential elements of understanding how you come across to them. Once you know this, you can start to think about adapting your behaviour so that their perception of you is what you want it to be. To feel confident, you need to know how you look and sound; you need to know how you come across. You need to know how to control people's perceptions of you.

> to feel confident, you need to know how you look and sound

Does it really matter what others think of you?

'Who cares what people think of me!' These might sound like the words of a confident person and to an extent the person is right to think like that. It's true that confident people don't worry as much as others might about what people think of them and how they come across. It's fine to think like this and be independent minded but it's dangerous to discount other people's perceptions of you completely.

To feel truly confident, it's important to understand the concept of perception and to take account of it when communicating. You need to be aware of people's perceptions of you but not let this cloud your judgement. If you let the concept of perception get the better of you, you could start to become paranoid.

People who disregard others' perceptions of them are missing a trick. It really does matter what people think and how they perceive you – but it shouldn't be the be all and end all. The reality of life is that most people can't help but be affected by other people's impressions of them and therefore how people react to them. This in fact is a positive thing if considered constructively. The important point to remember is that if you can control others' perceptions of you, you can control how they react to you.

Bear in mind that it can work the other way too. Most people who lack self-confidence make the presumption that people *perceive* them to lack confidence because of the way they look and act. This is not necessarily the case. Other people may in fact see you as a confident person! So – keep an open mind.

 **example**

Claudette

Claudette walked into the room at the beginning of a confidence-building course. She sat down and looked comfortable straight away, even though she hadn't met any of the other people there before.

Each person introduced themselves and explained why they had come. Claudette explained very confidently that she had no self-confidence at all. She said she felt embarrassed whenever she had to talk to a group of people. She actually said 'This is a great example … You can see it for yourself by the way I look now … I'm just a bag of nerves.'

We then discussed how the group perceived each person in terms of self-confidence when they introduced themselves. Claudette was staggered to hear that, without exception, all the people in the room perceived her to be a confident person. She genuinely could not believe it. She thought people were trying to be kind because, really, they thought she was so awful. She'd built up such a strong false impression of how she looked and sounded that it took quite a while for us to convince her that we weren't trying to be nice – we were telling the truth.

Claudette was just one of many people I meet who've formed the wrong perception of themselves.

Try thinking of the perception process as shown in Figure 4.1. If you can control people's perception of you, you can make it work in your favour. In other words, if you can ensure that their perception is positive, they'll see you as a confident person; if you interpret their reaction to you as positive, interested, motivated, animated … your confidence levels will rise – and of course it works the other way round too.

> if you can control people's perception of you, you can make it work in your favour

Imagine you're telling someone a story and in the middle they start yawning. This is bound to have an impact on you – after all,

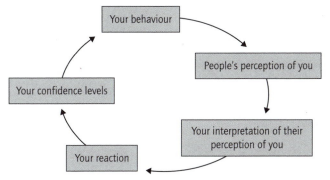

Figure 4.1 Perception process

to most people, yawning indicates boredom or lack of interest. If someone's expression suggests something negative about you, then this is bound to have an effect on your thoughts and behaviour – so for this reason it does matter what people think of you.

Confident people know how to process this negative information and how to react to it. They don't let this affect their *feelings*. If you can control your reaction so that it doesn't affect your emotions, then you can channel your efforts more effectively into dealing with the situation and being perceived as confident and in control.

So, if someone starts yawning when you're talking to them, it means something! You need to make a decision – if what you're telling them is important, you need to adapt your behaviour; you need to do something different because they're probably not listening properly. Some people find it helpful to say to themselves, 'I won't accept yawning when I'm talking to you.' This may sound a bit mad but it actually does work. It spurs you on to deal with the negative behaviour with confidence. Be careful though – make sure you don't say it out loud or it might backfire on you!

brilliant tip

Don't panic when someone appears to react negatively towards you. The situation can always be retrieved. Try to reflect, control your emotions, think positively and act with self-confidence.

Thick skinned?

Most people accept that other people's perceptions of them do matter.

Not all people though. Some people think that what others think of them is of no consequence at all. After all, 'confident people do their own thing'. They're right to some extent – however, they're not being very *clever*. Some might even say they're being over-confident – and that's dangerous territory to be in.

These people tend to be people we would describe as 'thick skinned'. They're just not bothered about what people think of them. Sometimes they even pride themselves in having this trait, this supposed 'strength of character'. It's true that they're lucky they don't get affected emotionally by what other people think of them – but, be under no illusion, that's where the benefit of being thick skinned stops.

 **example**

David

David seemed like a very confident person. He spoke clearly and had no problem sharing his thoughts. We were talking during a coaching session about the concept of perception and how it related to self-confidence.

Pretty well before we'd even started, David blurted out that he just couldn't see the link between the two. As far as he was concerned 'It didn't matter a damn what other people think of you … Surely confident people shouldn't be affected by other people's perceptions of them.'

David was a thick skinned person. He couldn't see that, although other people's perceptions don't affect the way *he* behaves, they do affect the way *others* behave towards him. Slowly, as we talked, he started to think about the possible implications of his disregard for other people's perceptions of him.

He'd worked as a security officer at an airport. He'd been performing the same role for six years and was keen to move into the operations team at the airport. He'd been telling his boss this for nearly six years. He knew there were opportunities to change role because he'd seen positions advertised on the internal email system. Eventually he started getting very frustrated because each time he asked his boss if he would put him forward, his boss told him he didn't think he would be 'suitable'. David couldn't work out what he meant.

▶

After a while he decided to take things into his own hands and he applied for one of the new roles. He thought he'd done well at the interview and was shocked to hear subsequently that he'd been unsuccessful. The feedback from the interview was that his 'strong personality' didn't suit the new role; furthermore, they felt he hadn't listened to the questions properly before answering.

During our discussion, the penny started to drop for David. Only now did he realise that others perceived him to be 'cocky', 'inconsiderate', 'insensitive', 'selfish' and 'arrogant'. He was genuinely shocked to hear this. In fact, it started to dawn on him that his failure to take account of others' perceptions was impacting on the path of his life. He'd failed the interview as a result of it.

brilliant tip

Have the confidence to 'do your own thing' but *don't* disregard other people's perceptions of you. Factor this into your thought processes and actions. Take account of people's perceptions but don't let this turn into paranoia.

Seeing how others perceive you – any surprises?

What determines how people perceive you? Knowing the answer to this question is the first step towards making sure that someone's perception of you is the perception you want them to have.

We take in so many different messages while we're forming a perception of someone. Some messages are obvious to the eye or ear – for example, if someone quite obviously stutters as they speak and has a weak voice, you tend to form the perception that they are nervous or uncomfortable.

Obvious physical messages like nervousness in your voice are relatively easy to address, mainly because you are already aware of them – after all, if you know you're doing something wrong, it's just a case of working out how to do it right, and then putting it into practice. (We'll cover ways of stopping yourself sounding nervous later.)

It's the other more subtle messages that can be difficult to identify and, therefore, to address: the way you stand, your eye contact, the tone of your voice, your natural expression … and the list goes on. We all have subtle behaviours that we have no idea we are portraying. These behaviours communicate underlying messages that we have no idea we are sending. Some of these work in your favour – you might describe them as positive behaviours – for example,

> we all have subtle behaviours that we have no idea we are portraying

if you have a posture which is naturally upright and open, you portray confidence. So this helps you to achieve what you want from the perception people have of you.

Other behaviours aren't helping you at all though. It's these negative behaviours that need to be identified and addressed. People who are perceived by others as confident are good at this. They have an awareness about their behaviour. They know they are vulnerable to certain negative behaviours and they keep on top of them.

So, by now, you're probably wondering how you find out if you personally have any negative behaviours and habits that affect people's perception of you – well, if you're not, you should be!

Identifying negative perceptions

There's one obvious way to establish if you're doing anything negative and that's to ask people. We'll come back to this later. I'd like you to try something else first.

Have you ever tried to compare your perception of yourself with the perception others have of you? This can be quite a revelatory exercise because people are often surprised to find that the two don't always match up. So, before you find out how other people perceive you (and before you start to cloud your own judgement with their perceptions), try this exercise.

 **brilliant** exercise

Self-perception

Try coming up with your own perceptions of yourself. To do this, you'll need to write down every adjective that comes to mind when you describe yourself. You need to be comprehensive when you do this – be honest. This should be a private exercise, not to be shared with anyone else; that way you won't have to worry about the embarrassment of what others might think – being straight with yourself shouldn't be a problem.

It's important to consider all aspects of your life. This is because words that you use to describe yourself at work don't necessarily come to mind when you're describing yourself at home or when you're socialising.

You need to cover what you consider to be both *good* and *bad* about yourself. So, make two lists – one for the negative descriptive words and the other for the positive words. Take your time over this. Make sure you cover everything. Don't make the mistake some people make – they forget to write down the good points! No one will see what you write so there's no chance anyone will think you're boasting.

These two lists you've created are going to form a focus for you as you read on. We'll use them as a means of building on your strengths and dealing with your weaknesses. So don't lose them! You'll need them later.

One thing to say first though – your aim will be to eliminate the bad words – the negatives. No longer can you have these negative perceptions of yourself. Confident people only allow positive perceptions. This doesn't of course mean that confident people are perfect – nobody is perfect. It's just that confident people have the strength of mind to overcome any negative perceptions and deal with them before they have an impact.

no longer can you have these negative perceptions of yourself

Don't forget, too, that some people form completely the wrong perception of what others around them think of them. In time, this can cause major problems if left to get out of control.

 **brilliant** example

Sachin

Sachin was of Indian origin. His family educated him in the Middle East. He'd made the most of the opportunity and had left university with a first class degree in Economics. Having graduated, he returned to India and was employed by a well-known international bank.

Life was going well for Sachin. He had got married and had two children. By now he'd been working for the bank for six years and had responsibility for a team of 40 people. The bank saw him as a rising star. They offered him a role in the UK to build a new team with the same role as his Indian team. He decided to take it because it was another step on his career path. Also, the salary was better and he felt he could offer his family a better standard of living in the UK.

So the family emigrated and moved into a rented flat just outside London while they looked for a house to buy. Sachin began his new job but very quickly started to feel uncomfortable. His colleagues were very different to those in India. Whereas in India he had been the boss, now he worked on a par with people. He wasn't used to that.

Sachin described his discomfort as a feeling of 'inferiority'. He couldn't think of anything specific that was causing this feeling, even when pushed. More and more he formed the impression that he was 'inferior' to others around him, even though he was better qualified and more experienced ▶

than most of them. He didn't feel there was anything racist about it, in fact the people he worked with were very nice. Eventually, he became demotivated and depressed. His work started to suffer and he struggled to recruit and build his team. The bank then demoted him.

We established during our discussion that Sachin had created this problem himself. With no substance at all to form a rational judgement, his perception of others had got the better of him. He'd found himself in a different culture to the one he was used to; people would approach him more directly and on occasions challenge him. This wasn't to check if he was good enough; it was just the way the UK operation worked. He wasn't used to this and as a result his perceptions of his colleagues were wrong in relation to the way they interacted with him. This caused his feeling of inferiority which eventually turned into an inferiority complex. It was totally unfounded because not only was he better qualified and more experienced than every one of his close colleagues, he was also studying for a Masters degree in his spare time.

Sachin lost all his confidence. This was incredibly frustrating and confusing because he knew that once, not so long ago, he had been a confident person. It went from bad to worse because his feelings of inferiority started to show themselves outwardly and eventually his colleagues (through no want or motivation of their own) started to view him and treat him as inferior.

He ended up moving jobs and accepted that he would have to take a cut in salary. He needed a change. It did him the world of good because it helped him to make a fresh start. With the help of personal counselling, he realised that his perception had got the better of him. It was totally wrong. He just needed someone to *tell* him. The difficulty had been that his feelings of inferiority had started to snowball once his mind turned negative. He saw everything negatively, even though, now that he looked back, he realised that a lot of the things that happened were in fact positive on his part in terms of his dealings with colleagues. He just couldn't see it at the time.

brilliant tip

Perception works in many ways. What you perceive of others is just as important as what they perceive in you. Don't make any assumptions – question your judgement regularly. If in doubt, think positively.

Inferiority

Sachin's perception of inferiority was specific to him. However, it does reflect a more wide-ranging problem. I find one of the main reasons people lack self-confidence is that they see around them a completely different world to the real one. They see the world as a place where everyone else is superior to them. They make the assumption that other people have more authority than them and that others' rights prevail above theirs.

It may well be the case that some people are more 'senior' to you in terms of position or rank. However, this does not mean that they are 'superior' to you in the sense that their rights and needs are more important.

Confident people treat everyone the same, regardless of rank or seniority. Of course, they show the appropriate degree of respect to seniors but they don't change their behaviour. People who feel inferior tend to lose sight of this. They forget that senior people have no 'rights' over you, even though, particularly in a work environment, they may have a degree of 'power' over you in terms of your role and responsibilities.

> confident people treat everyone the same, regardless of rank or seniority

brilliant tip

Always remember that you are on a par with everyone else.
Be professional and polite and try to treat everyone the same.
Approach a senior person with the confidence you would approach
a peer.

I wouldn't be surprised if you're thinking that's easier said than done. After all, it's natural to feel a little daunted by the prospect of treating people who are senior to you as equals. It's actually not that difficult – but it does require mental preparation. The following exercise should help.

brilliant exercise

Equal terms

Think forward to the next time you might find yourself working or socialising with a group of people, some of whom are senior to you in some respect. Prepare yourself to treat them differently to the way you might normally. Whereas you used to treat them according to your perception of their authority in relation to you, now you will treat each of them as an equal. You will do this for everyone, even the people who are more 'senior' to you in terms of position. Don't worry, this won't be a problem as long as you're polite and respectful at all times.

You'll be amazed at how this simple concept can transform your sense of inferiority into a feeling of equality. You'll also be pleasantly surprised at the more positive way people respond to you, even the more senior people.

Sachin made a number of misjudgements on what others thought of him. His issue was inferiority. In another situation

I've experienced, the issue was ugliness. I was coaching a person who thought she was ugly. Over the years, more and more, she managed to convince herself that she was ugly. Because she was so set in her mind regarding her self-perception, she then made the assumption that people's behaviour towards her always suggested that they thought she was ugly (when in fact they weren't thinking anything of the kind).

The ridiculous thing was that, to me, she seemed very attractive. I had to be careful how I told her this though!

Just ask!

Most people do wonder what people think of them every now and then. We've established that there's nothing wrong with wondering this. Actually, being aware of other people's perceptions of you is a vital component of feeling confident – it certainly doesn't mean you're vain or paranoid.

Have you ever taken it a step further and actually *asked* someone what they think of you? Not in terms of your morals or values, but in terms of how they perceive you specifically with regard to your confidence levels. You must try this – it's an essential crossroads on the journey to increased confidence.

 **exercise**

Straight talking

Consider what you can learn from others' perceptions of you. Overcome your inhibitions and ask a person you know well to give you some honest feedback. Prepare how you're going to ask before you approach them – because of most people's nature, they'll want to be nice to you; they'll probably be reluctant to hurt your feelings.

So, make sure they know you're serious about getting some constructive feedback. Tell them why you want the feedback. Tell them they aren't going ▶

to hurt your feelings if they have negative things to say – equally, tell them they aren't going to embarrass you if they have good things to say.

Ask them confidently – don't start giggling or looking embarrassed. Ask them if they think you seem like a confident person; and if not, why not. If yes, why yes? You're looking for advice on your behaviour, your body language and your verbal language. You may well be surprised at what you hear – many people are. Hold yourself back if you disagree with them – don't forget, they are being honest with you. They can't help what they see in you.

You might consider asking them if they would like some feedback too – on your perception of them. If you're honest with them, they'll be honest with you. Be careful though if you do offer, because while some cultures are very open and accepting in their approach to receiving personal feedback, others are incredibly sensitive. You could cause offence in some cultures unless you approach it carefully.

There's another way of finding out people's perceptions of you too:

 **exercise**

The Think Confidence Reality Check

On our website (**www.thinkconfidence.com**) you can find out how others perceive you by asking them to complete our Think Confidence Reality Check. They'll give you feedback by completing an online questionnaire anonymously – their names won't appear, so you won't know who said what.

It's a great way of finding out how others perceive you in terms of how you come across. You'll need to nominate people who you think you know well enough to give you some balanced feedback. The Reality Check is comprehensive. It covers everything from people's first impression of you to whether or not people think they can depend on you.

Try to choose as wide a range of people as possible: good friends, members of your family, work colleagues, neighbours, etc. The more people the better – that way you'll get a good overall impression of how people see you. Make sure people know they're completing the questionnaire anonymously – they're more likely to record what they really think. They'll also see this when they read the instructions for completing the Reality Check on the website.

The Reality Check will only work if people are completely open and honest in their answers. Replies are collated confidentially online through the Think Confidence website and sent to you by email. You won't know who gave which replies about you, but you will gain a great insight into how others perceive you.

If you'd like to read more about the Think Confidence Reality Check, go to **www.thinkconfidence.com/questionnaires.html**.

Filming

Being filmed is a great way of learning about how people see you. I always offer people who attend confidence-building courses the opportunity to be filmed. Very few people feel comfortable being filmed but, without exception, everyone finds it a revelatory exercise.

Receiving feedback verbally from people is very useful but there's nothing quite like seeing yourself in the flesh. It's interesting because pretty well everyone I film finds the exercise itself to be a confidence boost! Yes, I really mean this. People surprise themselves by coming across better than they thought they would. This is because most people have already *presumed* they'll look and sound awful. But it just doesn't work out like that. For example, it's often the case that people who thought they surely must have sounded very nervous realise that in fact they didn't sound nervous at all! It's also common for people who thought they waffled to see that in fact, they spoke clearly and didn't waffle at all!

most people sound and look better than they thought they would

Don't get me wrong here. I'm not saying that everyone I film is brilliant at it – of course not. But what I'm saying is that most people sound and look better than they thought they would. They genuinely surprise themselves and this boosts their confidence immediately.

Of course, you don't have to pay for a training course in order to be filmed. Some people film themselves privately. Make sure you have a topic if you're going to do this. Prepare properly first. Or maybe you could ask someone else to film you (and give you some feedback at the same time). Perhaps you could combine this with a meeting you're going to or a presentation you're giving at work. Film yourself as you practise your presentation – it's a great way to rehearse too.

Being aware

Stay aware all the time. Don't ever switch off to how others might be perceiving you. You can learn a tremendous amount by just watching how people behave towards you and by listening to what they say and the way they say it.

Watch people's expressions and their body language. Listen to what they say to you and the questions they ask. It could be a very simple question that people ask you regularly which you hadn't even thought significant that gives away their perception of you. For example, if people ask you if you're 'OK' a lot, it probably means you don't look OK to them! You must be doing something for them to form that perception.

Any adjustments required?

Already in *Brilliant Self Confidence*, you've worked through a number of exercises. They'll all help to boost your confidence levels. You've probably also identified a number of things you would benefit from doing differently. In other words, you need to make some changes. This means making some adjustments to the way you behave. There are some simple things you can do to make this process as smooth as possible.

To feel confident and in control from this point on in your life you'll need *self-discipline*.

Don't let the 'gremlin' get you!

The gremlin is behind that tempting feeling you get every time you either feel lazy, you procrastinate or you half-do something. Think back here to the 'stumbling blocks' exercise you completed (in Chapter 1). You listed the situations you find difficult to deal with. Your gremlin will be having a field day when this happens. Your gremlin has won when it stops you doing something you know you should do.

The gremlin is the cause of many things relating to your lack of self-belief, self-esteem and self-confidence. For example:

- Your gremlin is to blame for trying to pull you back during those situations when you know you *should* actually be putting your view across confidently.

- Your gremlin will be trying to get in your way when a job comes up at work that you know you *should* do but don't feel comfortable doing.

- Your gremlin will be trying to hold you back when an opportunity arises that you haven't quite got the confidence to seize.

This gremlin can massively affect the way you come across to people. If you let it get the better of you, you'll be seen as a person who is at best unhelpful and at worst lazy and not worth having in the team. The knock-on effect of this on your self-confidence could be catastrophic.

Remember, your gremlin *is not your friend* and nice to have by your side to help you stay out of the limelight, or to make you feel better if you feel lazy. The gremlin is your enemy.

You will know the next time your gremlin tries to get you. Be aware it's happening and overcome it. It could be today, tomorrow or the next day. It could be at work or at home. Wherever and whenever it happens, don't let the gremlin get you. Dealing with the damaging influence of your gremlin is one of the keys to overcoming the personal stumbling blocks you identified.

> you will know the next time your gremlin tries to get you

Your gremlin never goes away completely but confident people know how to deal with it. They speak up when they've got something useful to say. They seize opportunities when they arise. They act when they know it's appropriate to do so. Self-discipline is the key to success here.

brilliant tip

Your gremlin is terrified of self-discipline, moral courage and organisation. Don't let it get you!

 **brilliant** recap

Chapter 4

- To feel and look confident, you need to find out how you come across to people.

- It's dangerous to discount other people's perception of you.

- If you can control others' perception of you, you can control how they react to you.

- Be wary that you can easily give people a negative perception of you.

- Find a way to establish how people see you. Ask them, complete the Think Confidence Reality Check, film yourself speaking.

- Don't let the gremlin get you!

How do you communicate?

We've established the importance of considering how you come across to others and the implications that differing perceptions can have. But when you drill down, what is it that people actually do that makes them *look* and *feel* confident? There's one word that sums this up in a nutshell – *communication*. This is the nucleus around which your ability to look, feel and be more confident revolves.

So far, we've looked at how your mindset can affect your behaviour and, to some extent, what you say – you'll remember Julie who was a negative thinker and said 'if only' a lot, and Costas who couldn't stop saying 'sorry'. What we haven't yet looked at is how you communicate.

You communicate in your own particular way – we all do. Over the years you've developed your own natural communication style. To feel confident and in control, you need to be aware of this style. It's essential that you know what's good and what's bad about it; in other words, you need to know your strengths and weaknesses in relation to how you communicate.

> you need to know your strengths and weaknesses in relation to how you communicate

Some people like to be the centre of attention and to talk; others prefer to watch from the sidelines and to listen. Decisions such as these are determined both consciously and subconsciously through your natural communication style. This style is your own personal way of communicating, the way you come across when you don't consciously think about it. It will suit certain situations but not others. That's why it's so important to get to the bottom of it. Otherwise, there's a good chance that, just by being your normal self and communicating in your natural way, without even realising it, you'll:

- make someone feel uncomfortable
- distract them from your message
- appear rude to them
- appear boring and uninterested
- look like a person who lacks confidence.

the secret is to think about adapting your style

Once you know your natural style, you can make sure these negative perceptions don't arise. The secret is to think about adapting your style when you find yourself in a situation it doesn't suit.

This is one of the main reasons why people lack confidence and self-belief – they don't know when or how to adapt their communication style.

What is *your* natural way of communicating?

Before you can work out how to adapt your style, you need to establish what type of style you have. You need to know if it's helping you or hindering you in relation to your self-confidence. We're going to look at this in more detail now.

Most people think 'communication' is merely about talking. It's not though: talking is just one element of what it means to communicate. Try thinking more widely now about the concept of communication. For example, have you ever considered that *how* you say something might be just as important as *what* you say?

There are numerous models and theories that can help to identify your personal communication style. *Brilliant Self Confidence*
keeps it simple and considers four different types of style.
Each of these has its own traits and typical communication
behaviours.

The four *Brilliant Self Confidence* communication styles are:

- Methodical
- Sensitive
- Up-front
- Animated.

Some people find that they see the traits of just one of these
styles very strongly in themselves. Others find that they lean
towards two of the styles. Others find that they don't have a
particular leaning and have a balance of all four styles in their
personal communication behaviour.

The aim here isn't to pigeon-hole you into one particular style
but more to open your mind to the different ways people communicate. This should help you to have the confidence to use
one of the styles you don't naturally lean towards when you're
dealing with certain people.

Regardless of the style you naturally tend to adopt, it's important to understand that there is no 'best' or 'worst' style; there's
no 'right' or 'wrong' style to have.
However, there is an 'appropriate'
style for certain situations. So, being
able to adapt your style is pivotal if
you want to come across as more confident and become more influential.

> there is no 'best' or
> 'worst' style; there's no
> 'right' or 'wrong' style
> to have

You wrote down two lists when you were establishing your
perception of yourself, one with positive descriptive words and
the other with negative words (in Chapter 4). You might find it

helpful to refer to these here. They should help you to identify your natural style.

The Think Confidence Communication Style Questionnaire

If possible you now need to visit the Think Confidence website (**www.thinkconfidence.com**) to complete your free Think Confidence Communication Style Questionnaire. This relates directly to the chart shown in Figure 5.1 and will help you to build a clearer picture of your natural communication style. The higher your points score for a particular style in the questionnaire, the more strongly you demonstrate the traits of that style in your natural communication behaviour. A high score would be considered as 11 or above.

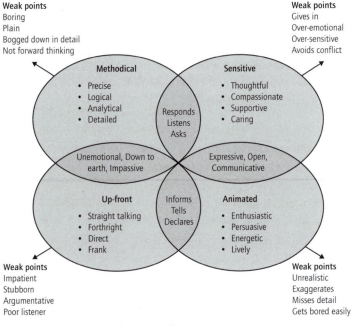

Figure 5.1 Communication style chart

If you don't have internet access, don't worry; just look at the chart and try to work out where your natural style fits best. You know yourself better than anyone so you should be able to be pretty accurate.

The chart shows four style sectors: methodical, sensitive, animated and up-front. The strengths of each style are bulleted within its sector. On the outside of the chart, the weak points of each style are shown.

Let's look at the strengths and possible weaknesses of each style in a little more detail. While reading this, you're interested as much in the style(s) you score high in as you are in the one(s) you score low in. That's because confident people have the ability to adopt the right style for the right situation. If you score low in a style, you'll need to start to learn how to use it because, at some point, it will be the style that suits best. We'll cover how you go about deciding this later.

Up-front style

Strengths

High scorers will look you in the eye and tell you what they think. They'll speak up forcefully when they have a point to make. They are decisive, will probably have a firm handshake and will walk with purpose. They like to get to the point, act and then move on.

Traits to watch out for (weak points)

High scorers think and talk in black-and-white terms. They may seem rude and too forthright to some people (particularly sensitive-style high scorers). They may fail to listen and to take account of other people's points of view. They could be prone to impatience, be argumentative and ignore advice.

Animated style

Strengths

High scorers tend to be enthusiastic people who have a lively character. They like to talk, can be quite persuasive and are interesting to listen to. They have an energetic way about them and, if very high scorers, are often the 'life and soul of the party'.

Traits to watch out for (weak points)

High scorers can sometimes get carried away with themselves in terms of their thoughts and their excited behaviour. They think in terms of generalities rather than detail and practicality. This can mean that they exaggerate and that their ideas may verge on the unrealistic. They may also appear overdramatic, particularly to methodical people, who tend to be more down to earth in their approach.

Sensitive style

Strengths

High scorers have a genuine interest in others. They communicate this through their words and through their receptive body language. They are good listeners and have a considerate nature. They are often softly spoken and patient and will express their feelings freely. They value strong work and personal relationships.

Traits to watch out for (weak points)

High scorers tend not to like conflict. They'll try to avoid conflict in the hope that it will go away without them having to deal with it. They might even give in rather than let the conflict continue. When they feel strongly about something, they can be quite emotional and show their feelings very expressively. They can get distracted quite easily if conflict arises within a working relationship.

Methodical style

Strengths

High scorers like detail and order. They tend to be analytical and precise in the way they think and speak. They like to base their opinions on facts and practicalities rather than concepts. They may be quiet in character but when they speak they're normally worth listening to because they've thought carefully about what they're going to say.

Traits to watch out for (weak points)

High scorers have a tendency to get bogged down in detail and lose sight of the longer-term perspective. They tend to think on a day-to-day basis rather than strategically. They don't display much emotion and aren't very expressive. They can appear to some people (particularly animated-style high scorers) as boring or uninterested whereas, in fact, they are neither.

Overlaps

You'll also see on the Communication Style Chart that there are areas of overlap between style sectors. These show the behaviours that are common to both styles.

Methodical/sensitive

If you score mainly across the top of the chart, in the methodical and sensitive sectors, your tendency is to want to listen, ask and then respond. In other words, you prefer to wait for the other person to speak before you do. You might even describe yourself as shy if your scores are high.

Up-front/animated

If your scores orientate towards the bottom two sectors of the chart, your tendency is to talk rather than to listen. In fact, if your scores here are high, you probably don't listen much at all. Your natural inclination is to deliver your opinion before hearing what others have to say.

Sensitive/animated

Scoring to the right of the chart suggests you are open in the way you communicate. It's probably quite easy for others to tell how you're feeling because you don't mind expressing your emotions. If you score very high in these sectors, you probably find your emotions getting the better of you on occasions.

Methodical/up-front

Scoring to the left of the chart suggests you prefer to keep your cards close to your chest. You tend not to be emotional and can perhaps be difficult to read. It's not that easy for others to tell what you're thinking or how you're feeling because you don't give much away through your body language or in terms of what you say.

Using the Think Confidence Communication Style Questionnaire effectively

Completing the Communication Style Questionnaire is an important step forward in your Self-Confidence Project. You should feel more confident now that you know your strengths and you should feel in a stronger position to address your weaknesses. However, there's much more than just this to be gained from this knowledge.

To *really* use your natural communication style effectively, you'll need to open your mind a touch. People tend to be most comfortable talking to or working with people who have a similar communication style to them. That's because people who communicate like you behave in a way that you can relate to. They do the things you do and don't distract you or frustrate you by communicating in a way that you don't like.

The problems tend to arise when you're dealing with someone who has a different style to you. You've probably heard the phrase 'personality clash' many times – what people often actually mean is 'communication style clash'. Understanding your natural communication style is the first step to dealing with this.

You should by now have either completed the Communication Style Questionnaire or had a good look at the Communication Style Chart to discover your own style. Now you can think constructively about when and how to adapt it so that you can come across confidently and assertively.

Style clashes

The degree to which your style might clash with someone else's tends to depend on how strongly you portray that style. For example, it wouldn't be at all surprising if a high-scoring methodical-style person sometimes feels uncomfortable interacting with a high-scoring up-front person. This is because methodical people like detail, they like to consider the whole picture, they tend to listen before speaking, they're not very expressive and they would prefer to take their time to check things. Up-front people are very different: they are more forthright, they speak before listening or asking, they can be impatient, they get bored with detail and they tend to be louder and more imposing.

This is just one example of a style clash. There are many more, depending on the styles involved. When you look at the differences between the styles on the Communication Style Chart, it's not difficult to see the reasons why styles clash if neither person makes any effort to adapt.

So, having established your natural communication style, you're in a stronger position to use this knowledge to come across more confidently. Try to start thinking along the following lines:

- Be prepared to adapt your style when you're talking to someone.
- You're not 'giving in' when you decide to adapt, you're being clever.

- Don't *expect* the other person to adapt – they may have no knowledge of the communication style concept, so don't blame them.

Approach every situation positively and take it upon yourself to solve it.

Adapting and mirroring

'If you talk to a man in a language he understands, that goes to his head. If you talk to him in his language, that goes to his heart.'

Nelson Mandela

'Adapting and mirroring' is a great way to solve a communication issue and build rapport with other people quickly. It's a simple concept which involves watching, adapting to and then mirroring the other person's style and behaviour. It's absolutely true that the more you can mirror their communication style, the more comfortable they will feel in your presence.

To make this work, you'll need to increase your state of awareness. You'll need to be more observant when you're talking to people. You're trying to take in as much as you can, as quickly as you can, about their verbal and non-verbal behaviour. You're looking at the other person's body language, facial expressions, tone, pace, volume of voice, energy level, enthusiasm, expressiveness and emotion.

> you'll need to be more observant when you're talking to people

In fact, what you're doing is trying to identify their communication style. Ideally, you'll be able to gauge roughly where you think the person would fall on the Communication Style Chart. Once you've worked this out, you can start to think about how similar, or perhaps different, their style is to your natural style. The more different they are, the more you'll need to adapt.

Of course, there will be some people who have a similar style to you. You probably won't have to adapt a great deal, perhaps even at all, to mirror these people. It's the people who have different styles to you that you'll need to work hardest on. Don't forget the Communication Style Questionnaire when you're thinking this through. If you judge that the other person would score high in the questionnaire in a different style to you, the 'clash' could be quite significant. This could be even more pronounced if you yourself score low in their style.

So, when using the Communication Style Chart concept to feel and look more confident, your senses have to detect when you're dealing with someone who has a strong natural communication style that's different to yours. Be prepared for this and bear in mind that you'll find it harder to mirror the other person's style if you personally don't like it, feel comfortable with it or use it naturally. Bear in mind also that the higher you score in your own style, the more unnatural it will feel to mirror someone who is different to you.

brilliant tip

Be careful how you do this: I'm not talking about mimicking the other person's behaviour – you've gone way too far if you do this and you'll start to look silly. Mirroring behaviour has to be done subtly for it to be effective.

To give you a better feel for how to put the concept of adapting your style into practice, here are some examples of people who have employed it successfully.

 **brilliant** example

Gethin

Gethin completed the Communication Style Questionnaire. His results showed the following scores for the four communication sectors:

- Methodical – 7
- Sensitive – 13
- Up-front – 4
- Animated – 4

This proved to be a useful exercise for Gethin. He began to realise why he didn't feel comfortable with certain people. There was one person in particular who he struggled with. When he thought about it, he came to the conclusion that this person (Aisha) probably scored high in the up-front sector on the chart. Whereas Gethin (sensitive sector score 13) was a caring person who was prepared to listen and take account of Aisha's thoughts and concerns, Aisha was a forthright, loud and, in Gethin's eyes, formidable person who didn't listen or show any interest in his point of view.

Gethin made a conscious decision to adapt in order to mirror Aisha's style the next time they met. Whereas before he had let her dominate the conversation, this time he looked her in the eye, spoke louder than normal, didn't waffle and explained his thoughts clearly and concisely. Having scored 13 in the sensitive sector, Gethin didn't find this easy to do because adapting meant behaving very differently to his natural preferred style. It worked brilliantly for him though.

He walked away from the meeting feeling that he had achieved what he wanted. Subsequently, with his new-found confidence, Gethin was able to talk openly to Aisha about how he had found the Communication Style Chart concept useful in terms of his working relationship with her. He was surprised to hear that she actually preferred him to be more up-front and found it easier to work with people like that! It was lucky she told him because, up to then, he'd thought that being so forthright with someone would surely sound rude or aggressive.

Gethin's decision to adapt to the up-front style worked well when dealing with Aisha. It wouldn't work though if he used it for someone who scored high in one of the other three styles.

brilliant tip

Remember to keep an open mind when using the Communication Style Chart concept. What works for one person might not work for another.

brilliant example

Ellen

Ellen completed the Communication Style Questionnaire and scored as follows:

- Methodical – 5
- Sensitive – 6
- Up-front – 5
- Animated – 12

It had puzzled her why some people just didn't seem to take her seriously. It had never occurred to her that it might be something to do with her natural style. Ellen was a very expressive person who liked talking and tended to exaggerate. She liked to talk about ideas and got bored easily with any discussion that involved day-to-day practicalities.

She was so lively and enthusiastic about everything that some people found this completely over the top and unbearable. Ellen found this confusing because she thought these were positive traits. She even thought to herself on occasions, 'If everyone was as fun and lively as me, the world would be such a great place – some people are just so boring.'

Ellen thought about her friends and work colleagues and tried to place each one of them in the Communication Style Chart. She started to see that ▷

the people she got on best with were the people who fell in the animated sector; in other words, she got on best with people who thought, talked and approached life like she did.

What she also started to see was that the people she clashed with tended to be the opposite to her. For example, she found one person (Susie) incredibly frustrating because she never showed any emotion. Susie always had the same expression and never seemed to get excited about anything – even good things. It got to the point where Ellen couldn't help seeing Susie as a negative person. What's more, Susie seemed paranoid about detail – everything had to be organised and in the right place.

Ellen was pretty certain that Susie would score high as a methodical-style person on the chart, the direct opposite to her own style. So she started to think about what she might need to do to mirror Susie's style. Thinking this through made her realise that, actually, Susie wasn't a negative person, she just communicated and behaved differently to her. Although it was a huge effort (because her own style was so strong and so different to Susie's), Ellen vowed that she would try to mirror Susie's methodical style when she was dealing with her in future.

She did this by trying to control her emotion and to temper her loud and lively approach when she was with Susie. She also made a conscious effort not to get carried away with her ideas and to forget to ask and then listen to Susie's thoughts. She had to remind herself to have a structure to what she was saying so that Susie didn't think she was waffling. This helped her to cover the level of detail that Susie liked.

These simple changes in the way Ellen behaved made a huge difference, not just for her relationship with Susie but also for her self-confidence. She noticed that the people who used not to take her seriously started to ask her opinion more and listen more attentively to what she was saying.

Whereas Gethin found it helpful to project himself and talk more, Ellen found that she needed to temper her desire to speak and to try to listen more. Decisions like these can only be made by weighing up the differences between your style and the styles of the people around you.

 **brilliant** tip

Keep an open mind and treat each person as an individual when deciding which style best suits.

 **brilliant** example

Matt

Matt scored as follows in the Communication Style Questionnaire:

- Methodical – 7
- Sensitive – 7
- Up-front – 7
- Animated – 7

Matt's scores were balanced throughout the sectors. My experience is that Matt falls into a small minority of people who don't have a leaning towards one or two of the styles. In some ways Matt is lucky because he doesn't have to make the adjustment others need to make in order to mirror someone else's style. After all, having the same score throughout indicates that Matt naturally portrays all the styles in a measured way.

However, he shouldn't be complacent; he still needs to consider the styles of people around him. Just like everyone else, he needs to identify the style he needs to mirror. Just being his normal self might not be enough if the other person strongly displays the traits of a particular style. He'll need to adapt so that his style matches the strength of the other person's.

brilliant tip

If you complete the Communication Style Questionnaire and find your scores are fairly balanced, you'll still need to have the awareness and confidence to pick which style best suits the situation.

brilliant recap

Chapter 5

- Know your 'natural communication style'. What do you sound like and what sort of messages does your body language send out?

- Complete the Think Confidence Communication Style Questionnaire to find out. Are you Methodical, Animated, Sensitive or Up-front?

- Get your communication style wrong and you could put the person off straight away.

- Once you know your style, you can start to think about when and how to adapt it to get the result you want.

- Treat each person you interact with as an individual with a style of their own. Could you come across more confidently and assertively with them if you adapted your style to match theirs?

Putting self-confidence into action

Why is assertiveness so important?

To be assertive is to influence

It's time to start thinking about putting your Self-Confidence Project into action. Part 3 of Brilliant Self Confidence bridges the gap between *thinking* about being more confident and actually *doing it*.

You'll see that the concept of assertiveness is a major component here. Some people find it hard to differentiate between assertiveness and confidence so let's clarify this straight away. We established at the beginning of *Brilliant Self Confidence* that confidence is a skill that relates to your attitude and your state of mind. Assertiveness is a skill too, but it relates to your behaviour rather than to your mindset. So, in short, confidence is a mental state and assertiveness is a behaviour. The important thing to acknowledge is that both are *skills* you can learn.

> confidence is a mental state and assertiveness is a behaviour

There's one major thing to remember here – self-belief and confidence *cannot* exist if you don't have the skills to be assertive. It's *that* important.

Confident people use assertive behaviour to influence others. *Influence* is having the power to affect someone's beliefs, actions or thought processes.

The chain is simple (see Figure 6.1).

Figure 6.1 The influence chain

Finding a balance

Truly assertive people have found that critical balance between stating their case and taking account of the views of the other person. They've acknowledged that their own needs, wants and rights are equally as important as the other person's.

Confident people are in a stronger position to be 'actively' assertive than those who lack confidence because they're more inclined to speak up. However, just because you're confident doesn't mean you can be truly assertive. For example: you might be good at stating your case, but can you listen?

Truly assertive people have found the balance; they aren't just able to present their own case – they also have the sensitivity and moral courage to accommodate the other person's case if necessary. They might even give in if they think the other person is right or has a better idea.

True assertiveness falls in the middle of two extremes. It keeps the seesaw balanced (see Figure 6.2).

People who use their self-confidence effectively are able to fine-tune the balance of the seesaw. They manage and control their behaviour so that it falls within the 'Control Zone' at

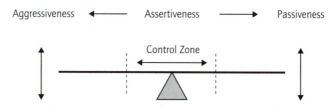

Figure 6.2 The assertiveness seesaw

all times. They understand that both passive (listening) and active (speaking) behaviour are required for true assertiveness. However, they also know that extreme behaviour in one or the other direction can unbalance the seesaw to such an extent that control is lost. Confidence levels can be severely dented if this happens.

Let's have a look at what extreme behaviour in either direction constitutes.

'Over-confident' people take note … It's great to be confident but be careful not to overdo it when you're being actively assertive. If you do, you may well be seen by some people as aggressive …

Aggressiveness

Aggressive people boldly insist that their rights, views and needs prevail.

They fall into two categories:

- Those who have an inflated ego and an unrealistic sense of self-importance.
- Those who use 'aggressiveness' as a way of hiding a deeper sense of insecurity or another weakness.

Whichever category they fall into, aggressive people express their feelings and opinions in a way that violates the rights of others. They have no consideration for others' opinions and, in extreme cases, will be verbally and/or physically abusive in order to get their way.

Aggressive people may get away with it in the short term but eventually their behaviour will have a negative impact on their self-confidence and self-belief.

 **example**

Pauline

Pauline was a newly qualified teacher in a secondary school. She'd just finished her first year there. She was told by her department head during her annual appraisal that she was perceived by both colleagues and students as 'aggressive'. She'd known for a while that something wasn't quite right with her approach and manner but she hadn't been able to put her finger on it. It wasn't until her boss explained it that she realised. Pauline thought she was being 'confident', not aggressive. She thought that it was part of a teacher's job to behave like that.

We talked about this during the confidence-building course she attended. It soon became clear to her that her behaviour was weighing down the aggressive side of the seesaw; the passive side was way out of reach and almost in the clouds. She was strong at putting her point of view across but couldn't see that others were feeling threatened by her behaviour. The pupils were scared to ask questions and her colleagues felt uncomfortable working with her.

She started to see that she was shutting out other people's views and needs. She'd genuinely thought she was an assertive person when, in fact, she was aggressive. She left the course with the aim of developing her passive side and her listening skills.

Pauline found the 'Turning the clock back' exercise (Chapter 1) very useful. She recalled a number of experiences she'd had. These experiences had led her to feel insecure and uncertain of herself. Her aggressive behaviour was actually a 'smoke screen' that she deployed to hide these hidden vulnerabilities. She'd become very adept at this, so good in fact that no one had any idea she was acting. So, aggression wasn't her natural behaviour at all; when she relaxed and we got to know her better, we started to see her passive side coming out.

Understanding the need to find the middle ground to achieve true assertiveness was a major step forward for Pauline. Whereas before she'd felt that revealing her passive side would make her more vulnerable, during the course she started to see that showing your passive side is a critical part of feeling and being confident.

So, ask yourself if any of the following words describe the way you behave or treat people:

Humiliate, dominate, criticise, blame, threaten, interrupt, order, shout, bully …

These are aggressive, not assertive behaviours. Don't be mistaken by thinking they are confident behaviours – they might seem confident in the simplest of senses but actually they'll work against you and hinder your self-belief and self-confidence eventually. You can't get away with behaving like this for ever. People just won't accept it.

Passive-aggressiveness

Passive-aggressive people get their way by subtle, underhand means.

This is a style of aggressiveness that a very small minority of people demonstrate. As the name suggests, passive-aggressive behaviour is a style that mixes passiveness with aggressiveness. People appear passive on the surface but have an aggressive streak in their character. This aggressiveness isn't seen physically in the person's behaviour; they will strive to get what they want through subtle, indirect and hidden means. They will smile and look cooperative, but behind this veil they'll be plotting and scheming to get their way.

This behaviour goes completely against the concept of assertiveness because it is not *open*. Assertive people create a two-way dialogue which takes both people's viewpoints, feelings and needs into consideration. People who act in a passive-aggressive way tend to behave as they do because they feel incapable of dealing directly with people. They lack the courage.

Passive-aggressive people will use facial expressions that don't match how they feel, they'll smile when they're angry, they're often sarcastic and they'll deny there's a problem when they know there is one.

 **example**

Ted

Ted used to be a work colleague of mine. Although I tried, I never really got on with him all that well. I thought it was just because we approached problems differently and didn't have the same interests. Eventually though, I worked out the real reason. Although I couldn't see it, it had been staring me in the face – he often used passive-aggressive behaviour.

Ted had a habit of letting people make mistakes when, all along, he knew they were doing the wrong thing. This wasn't because he was shy or afraid of embarrassing the person; he seemed to take pride in saying to people after the event, 'I could have told you that was going to happen' or 'I knew that was never going to work.'

This came to a head on one occasion when we were working on a project together. The project involved developing an online employee appraisal system. The client wanted the appraisal software to include a comprehensive analytics element that would allow them to download different types of reports on performance trends within their business. Ted was a technical expert on the software and knew its capabilities but he didn't have a direct role or responsibility for the reporting element itself.

The project went well all through the implementation stage and it wasn't until the first year's appraisals were completed that the problems started. It transpired that the system wouldn't allow the client to produce the type of reports they wanted.

When he heard about this, Ted wasted no time showing his passive-aggressive streak … he kept saying, 'I could have predicted that would happen.'

Thanks Ted.

Passiveness

Passive people don't express their own views and concede that other people's rights, views and needs prevail over theirs.

Passive people fall into two categories:

- Those who are too shy to voice their own opinions and needs.
- Those who are so 'nice' that they genuinely feel that other people's opinions and needs should prevail over theirs.

Whichever category they fall into, passive people avoid expressing their opinions or feelings, protecting their rights, and identifying and meeting their own needs. Passive people are the most likely to lack self-confidence in the obvious sense; they try to avoid the limelight and will often use their passive traits to achieve this. At the extreme, passive people give in and accommodate to such an extent that their opinions and needs are never heard, let alone considered.

 **example**

Steve

Steve attended a confidence-building course run in the training room at his office. I remember him well. He walked in quietly and sat down without saying a word, even though some others had already arrived and were in conversation.

The course started and a pattern started to develop. Steve would only speak when prompted and struggled to say anything meaningful whenever it involved giving his opinion. He even found it hard to commit himself when asked what time would suit him best for lunch. His first reaction to this question was to listen to what time would suit the other people. As a result, we had lunch at a time that was convenient for them, not him.

It transpired during the afternoon that Steve had missed an opportunity due to his passive approach. He'd known at the beginning of the day that ▶

a new client was visiting to meet his boss at 12.30. His boss had even said that it would be great if Steve could find the time to introduce himself.

So, even when the opportunity presented itself, Steve failed to speak up. If he'd said something, we could have arranged the lunch break to accommodate him (particularly as no one else had any reason to ask for a specific time!).

Steve was demonstrating typically passive behaviour. His first thoughts focused on other people's opinions and wants rather than his own. Steve was a thoroughly nice person but was making the mistake of thinking that he would 'hurt people's feelings' if he told them what he thought or what he wanted.

So, ask yourself if you do any of the following:

- give in easily
- struggle to communicate your needs and wants
- allow others to influence you when you know you're right
- fail to express how you feel
- speak quietly or apologetically
- feel shy and try to avoid being in the limelight
- think so much about others that your needs suffer
- do other people's work before your own
- say 'yes' *every time* someone asks you to do something for them.

If you find yourself falling into these traps, you're definitely being too passive.

Don't worry about putting your point of view across and standing up for yourself. As long as you present yourself politely and take account of what the other person is saying (and accommodate if appropriate), your request should be received in a positive way.

Assertiveness

Confident people manage to find the middle ground between aggressive and passive behaviour. That's because they're in *assertive territory* (see Figure 6.3).

Assertive people clearly express and take into account that other people have rights, views and needs. Assertive people are comfortable stating their case while at the same time being respectful of the viewpoint of others.

The term 'assertiveness' can sometimes be misunderstood. It's helpful to set aside some misconceptions before we move on. Let's firstly clarify what assertiveness is not.

Assertiveness is not about:

- trying to dominate
- being louder than others
- being popular
- taking charge.

Assertive people have the confidence and the skills to influence others. They achieve this in an open, polite, sensitive but

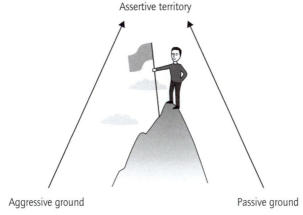

Figure 6.3 Assertive territory

authoritative way. They've found the right balance between passive behaviour (satisfying other's needs, wants and rights) and aggressive behaviour (demanding your own needs, wants and rights).

True assertiveness comes through confident, clear, calm and honest communication. Assertive people have the self-confidence to establish relationships in which everyone knows where they stand and everyone feels they have a say.

Balancing the bar

Have a look at the assertiveness seesaw below. Try to gauge where you think you fall on the bar. It's a simple but important exercise.

You might find it helpful to refer back to the two lists of adjectives you used to describe yourself (in Chapter 4). Reflect again on the lists. It could be that a passive or aggressive theme emerges for you.

Put a cross where you think you fall on the line in Figure 6.4.

There are a number of reasons why the seesaw tilts. A serious tilt can lead to a loss of control.

I find that a lot of people who attend my confidence-building courses find themselves leaning towards the passive side of the seesaw. The interesting thing is that the majority of these people already know this. They also know that there are times when

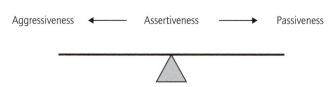

Figure 6.4 The assertiveness seesaw gauge

they need to be more direct and forthright in putting their point of view across. They just struggle to actually *do* it.

So, if you see yourself as passive, the first thing to accept is that *there is nothing wrong with being passive* – confident people can be passive but not to the extreme and not all the time. They know when a situation demands passive behaviour and will act passively to accommodate it. So don't fall into the trap of thinking your confidence levels are suffering because you're too 'nice' and 'accommodating'. You should be pleased you have this sensitive side to you – some people really struggle to find it.

I also find that very few people score themselves towards the left of the bar as aggressive. This doesn't necessarily mean I don't meet aggressive people though. It's just that aggression is often a characteristic that people can't see in themselves – they need to be told by others. The perception exercises you did (in Part 2) might have helped you here.

The trick is to make sure the seesaw doesn't over-balance. If you lean too much towards the aggressive side, you need to temper your behaviour so that people don't feel threatened by it. If you lean too much towards the passive side, you'll need to develop the confidence to stand up for yourself when appropriate.

So how do you find this critical balance? You've already taken the first step by identifying where your natural behaviour positions you on the seesaw. The degree to which you lean one way or the other will dictate how far you need to move to be truly assertive. You might even find that you're already fairly central on the bar. That doesn't necessarily mean that you've cracked it and have nothing more to do though. You've still got to physically demonstrate assertive behaviour and that means *engaging* people.

Assertive behaviour – the thinking side

Truly confident people have overcome any negative thoughts that may hinder their ability to be assertive. We know (from Chapter 2) that confident people always try to think positively. They also continually remind themselves that *they have as much right* as anyone else to speak. If you're a passive person, you'll need to work hard at this.

Don't fall into the trap of panicking unnecessarily about being assertive; I find that people who lack confidence tend to worry for no reason, particularly on the active side of assertiveness. They come up with all sorts of negative comments when trying to explain why they struggle to be actively assertive.

Let's deal with these straight away.

Here are some typical comments to the question: 'I don't like the idea of being assertive because …'

- *'People won't respect me'* – This couldn't be further from the truth. Try to think of people you know who speak their mind assertively. Do you disrespect them? I'd be very surprised if your answer is 'Yes'. My experience is that people have more not less respect for those who stand up for themselves and voice their opinion (as long as their message is presented politely). This is because you know where you stand with people who speak their mind.

- *'People will think I'm a negative person'* – They won't think you're a negative person as long as you use positive language to explain your position. Don't whinge, complain or criticise negatively. Don't make any presumptions regarding the assimilation of your message. Remember the lessons learnt about misinterpretation (in Chapter 4). If people know clearly the reasoning behind your point of view and the positives that may come from it, they shouldn't see you as a negative person.

- *'People will think I'm selfish'* – No one will think you're selfish if you show that you care. Yes, put your point of view across, but don't forget to show your passive side. People need to feel that you respect their opinion. To do this you have to let them share their thoughts with you. You also have to listen (we'll look in more detail at this later). Assertive people also keep an open mind – it could be that the other person says something that changes your opinion.

- *'People will think I'm a bully'* – They won't see you as a bully if you share your thoughts professionally and politely. Only aggressive people are seen as bullies. Your body language and physical presence make a massive difference here. We'll cover this in detail later in the chapter.

- *'People will dislike me'* – As long as you present your thoughts in a considered, sensitive and honest way (and not aggressively), most people would prefer to hear them than not. This is true even when they may disagree with you. They prefer to know what you're thinking rather than suspect that you're harbouring misgivings or not telling them something. They're more likely to dislike you for this than they are for presenting your thoughts to them confidently.

brilliant tip

Banish these demons. Don't forget – true assertiveness *requires* you to share your wants, needs and concerns. Assertive people know this and use it effectively to influence others.

Preparation

'One important key to success is self-confidence. An important key to self-confidence is preparation.'

Arthur Ashe, Wimbledon Men's Champion, 1975

Preparation requires time. Making time for yourself to prepare means being organised. It's easier to make time to prepare for planned events like meetings, social gatherings or presentations than it is for unforeseen events. The difference here is that for planned events the time is already available whereas for unforeseen requests you may have to *make the time available* to think about your answer.

Preparing a confident answer to an unforeseen request

Some people are very good at pressurising you into doing things you hadn't planned to do. They expect you to give them an answer there and then – they know what they want and they'll pile on the pressure to get it.

From now on, you're not going to let them get away with it. Make a pact with yourself and try not to break it. The key to not being pressurised into doing something is to delay your answer; think back to some of the things people have asked you to do recently – would delaying your answer have made a difference? Would you have given a different answer if you'd had a little time to think about it?

> very rarely does a request require an answer there and then

The vast majority of requests made of you won't be affected adversely if you give yourself a little time to think. Very rarely does a request require an answer there and then.

There are very few situations when it isn't possible to create this little window of opportunity to prepare your answer. Confident people are good at giving themselves time to think before they speak or act. This is vital if you're to come across assertively and credibly. If you have your wits about you, there *are* ways of creating time to prepare your answer even when someone approaches you and expects an answer there and then. If you can win a minute or two, that's potentially all you need.

So, how do you create this window of time and how can you best use that time?

Be alert at all times. Be ready for people who make requests or demands of you. If it's a work situation, you may already know people who continually ambush you and ask you to do things. They're not going to suddenly stop doing this for no reason – so, if you know it's going to happen at some stage during the day, get ready for it. Have a reply prepared. This will give you valuable thinking time and should stop you giving a 'knee-jerk' reply that you regret later.

Imagine then that I'm your boss and I stop you in the corridor. It's a busy day and you've got lots on your plate already. Out of the blue, I try to give you another job to be completed that day. What would your normal reply be? People who lack self-confidence tend to say 'Yes' and accept the task immediately; they don't want to let their boss down, be seen as negative, uncooperative, lacking motivation … and the list goes on.

Of course, there's a good chance that having added this extra job to your list, one of *your* jobs that you'd planned to do doesn't get done. As your boss, I won't know this but may well find out later and blame *you* for being inefficient!

Deciding whether it's a 'Yes' or a 'No'

People who lack confidence find themselves continually under pressure because they accommodate others and say 'Yes' whenever a request is made of them. They might be lovely, helpful people but the bottom line is that they can be terribly inefficient simply because they just can't say 'No'. The difficulty is that once you're seen by others as a 'Yes' person, you become a magnet for them. They'll turn to you first when they need something done. You then end up doing other people's jobs, not your own.

 **exercise**

Yes or No?

Think of people you know who have the confidence to say 'No' when appropriate. The term 'when appropriate' is important here – you're thinking of people who've achieved the right balance, i.e. people who say 'Yes' when they think it's right to do so, but also have the confidence to say 'No' too.

Now ask yourself – would you describe any of these people you've thought of as negative, uncooperative or selfish just because on occasions they say 'No' to a request? I would guess not, because they've got the balance right. They'll accommodate and help when appropriate and have the confidence to say 'No' when necessary.

So, try to remember – there's nothing negative about saying 'No'.

It's easy to get into the habit of saying 'Yes' but, with practice, you can get out of it by taking some simple steps:

1 Don't give the person an answer there and then (it may not seem possible but this *is* possible in 99 per cent of situations – you need to try it to find out).

2 Tell the person you need a little bit of time to consider their request. Try to grab as much time as possible. Even a few seconds is better than nothing. An hour or longer is ideal (by then they might have found someone else to do the job anyway). Make sure you tell the person when you will give them an answer.

3 During the time you've bought yourself, consider the following:

   ● Is this a job I should be doing or is this person just trying to get me to do it because they don't want to do it themselves?

- If the request is work related, does it fall under my role and responsibility? (It's helpful to have an up-to-date job description, otherwise you might struggle to come to a balanced decision here).

- If I say 'Yes', how will doing this extra job affect my other priorities?

- If I say 'No', how am I going to tell the person this confidently and sensitively?

These steps should help you to make a balanced decision. You might only need a couple of minutes or less to do this for simple requests. For more complicated requests, try to buy as much time as possible.

Don't make the mistake of thinking that 'confident' people say 'No' all the time – they don't. If a 'Yes' is warranted and the knock-on effect to your own priorities is manageable, try to accommodate the person. Do this on your terms though. For example, if there's a degree of flexibility on timings, suggest that you'll do the job when it suits *you*, not them.

The keys to saying 'No'

If a 'No' is warranted, there's an art to saying it. Don't go back to the person and simply blurt out 'No, I'm sorry I can't do that'. It might *sound* confident but it isn't clever. Believe it or not, there are ways of saying 'No' *positively*.

To achieve this, prepare your reply in three stages:

1 *Make a positive start* – Try to be sensitive and positive in your approach. i.e. '*I'd like to help* and I've thought carefully about your request but it's just not going to be possible this time because ...'

2 *Explain the reasons why* – Don't make the assumption that the person knows why you've decided to say 'No'. Explain your reasoning, i.e. 'If I do this for you now, I'm going

to let other people down due to other deadlines I have to meet'. It might help to be more specific than this so that the person understands the reality of your predicament.

If you don't explain your reasons, there's a good chance you'll be perceived as being negative – after all, you can't expect the person to guess why you're saying 'No'. If it's a request from your boss, there's another benefit of explaining your reasons for saying 'No'; if your boss decides to override this and 'orders' you to do it, your boss now knows which deadlines you're going to miss as a result. You can't be criticised later for this because you clearly explained the implications of you doing it at the beginning.

On the other hand, your boss may well say, 'OK, fine, don't worry then, I'll sort it out myself, I didn't realise how much you had on your plate.' If so, that's brilliant – you're in the clear!

3   *Suggest a possible solution* – Try to present the person with a possible solution that doesn't involve you. You might not be able to think of something every time but anything you can suggest that may help the person will be seen in a positive light, i.e. 'Have you thought about doing this/trying that/asking so-and-so ...?'

 **brilliant** exercise

No magnets

Have a go. Try practising these approaches straight away. Make sure you're alert the next time someone requests something of you out of the blue. Most people find that it happens more often than they realised (particularly at work). You'll be amazed at how often you find yourself using these techniques. Be prepared though - when you start using them, it might seem like 'preparation overkill' for a reply to a simple request. It's not though - once you try it, you'll get the feel of it. Once you get practised at it, you'll see that you can come up with a balanced reply in just a few seconds. Eventually, for smaller requests, you should be able to give a prepared answer there and then. No longer will you find yourself giving 'knee-jerk' answers which you subsequently regret.

Once you get into the habit of presenting your reasoning like this, people will start to see that the 'rules' have changed. No longer are you a 'Yes' person and therefore a magnet for people who are looking to spread their workload. As your colleagues, friends and relations get more and more used to this, they will change the way they treat you as a matter of course.

Here are some of the other benefits you can get from this simple concept of saying 'No' when appropriate:

- Your self-confidence starts to build.
- You can manage other people's requests rather than them managing you.
- You are *seen* to be a more confident person.
- You become more organised and better at managing your deadlines.
- People's respect for you grows because they know where they stand with you.
- You won't promise to do things that you then struggle to fulfil.
- You seize the initiative and take control.
- People only approach you when they have a relevant request.
- Your stress levels decrease because you're under less pressure.
- You end up doing your job rather than bits of everyone else's.

Preparing for a pre-arranged event

'If I had six hours to chop down a tree, I'd spend the first hour sharpening the axe.'

Abraham Lincoln

Preparing yourself in advance of the event is vital if you want to feel and look confident and in control when the event takes place.

Perhaps you've said 'Yes' to a request to give a presentation, play a part in a meeting or speak at a social engagement. Or maybe these types of events form part of your job or lifestyle anyway. Once more, good preparation could be the difference between success and failure. The better prepared you are, the more confident you'll feel.

the better prepared you are, the more confident you will feel

When you start your delivery on the day, you should already have a thorough knowledge of your message content and structure. People who feel and look confident when speaking have nailed this already. As a result they're able to focus their minds on the characteristics that confident people exude – charisma, enthusiasm, supportive body language and audience awareness.

With a pre-arranged event, you're in the lap of luxury of course with regard to preparation – whereas in the previous section you were preparing your answer to an unforeseen request and you only had a few minutes to decide whether your answer would be 'Yes' or 'No', now you've got time on your side.

So, whether or not you feel and look confident when the event takes place will depend very much on how well you prepare beforehand.

The 'W' concept

The following checklist is useful for all situations that involve you communicating information to others. They could be formal or informal situations at work or in your personal life – for example, meetings, presentations, social engagements, interviews and speeches.

Keeping your preparation method simple is essential. So ask yourself these four simple questions before you start to prepare the actual content of what you're going to say.

Why?

What am I trying to achieve? What is my objective? If *you* don't know what you're trying to achieve, nor will the person (or people) you're talking to. If you tend to waffle, setting yourself a clear objective will keep you on track. As you move on to prepare what you're going to say, reflect regularly on your objective – continually ask yourself: does this help me to achieve my objective or is it just waffle?

When deciding on your objective, ask yourself what you're aiming to achieve:

- Am I trying to persuade?
- Am I trying to sell?
- Am I trying to inform?
- Am I trying to explain?
- Am I trying to amuse?

Be crystal clear about what you want to achieve. Then tell the people right at the beginning what your objective is. Don't be frightened to do this. They'll immediately perceive you as confident and in control if you state right at the start what you aim to achieve (your body

be crystal clear about what you want to achieve

language must of course support this statement – we'll come to that later in the chapter). Everything you then say should relate to this objective and contribute in some way to its achievement.

Watch people sit up when you state your objective enthusiastically – it really works!

Who?

It's vital to do as much research as you can beforehand on who you're going to be talking to. You may know the people already but, even so, don't make any assumptions.

Ask yourself:

● Is it one person or a group (if so, how many)?

● What are their names, age bracket and backgrounds?

● If it's a work situation, what's the culture of their organisation?

● What do they need to know?

● What do they know already?

● What are their needs, concerns or sensitivities?

> confident speakers create a link with the person or group very quickly

Confident speakers create a link with the person or group very quickly. They show an awareness that an audience might not necessarily *expect*. This is what sets a confident speaker apart from the rest. You can't do this if you haven't done any research. People respect speakers who show they've made an effort to learn about them; someone who cares and has their interests at heart.

It's helpful to know how many people you'll be addressing. There are of course the obvious practical reasons for this – for example, the number of chairs, handouts etc. For me, though, the numbers are important for more subtle reasons. Knowing the number of people attending helps me to decide on my approach. I might run a meeting with a group of five or fewer people differently to a group of fifteen people – I might, for example, build in more 'discussion' time for the smaller group. In essence, I feel better prepared mentally if I know the group size beforehand – there are no 'shocks' in store.

Knowing their rough ages and a little about their backgrounds and experience can also help. For instance, you might consider dealing with a group of students differently to a group of directors.

Maintaining the group's interest and engaging them throughout is essential. You can only achieve this if you've thought about what they need to know, understood what they know already and considered their needs, concerns and sensitivities.

Finally, in the business context, researching the culture of the organisation and audience is also helpful. For example, you might choose to dress more smartly for one audience than another. This could make a real difference if, for example, you are a training consultant and looking to win a new training contract. The potential client will want you to fit in with their culture so that their delegates (i.e. the people you will be training) see you as credible and 'on their wavelength'; wearing a pinstripe suit to a meeting with a client in the arts field probably isn't going to send out the right message.

When?
This question is important in two respects:

- How much time is available for preparation?
- How much time is available for the delivery of your message?

If possible, give yourself more time than you think you'll need. I always try to have the preparation complete at least two days before the event. This may sound incredibly conservative and organised but it's worth the effort. It gives me time to reflect and relax while reviewing what I've prepared. I *always* change something to improve it or notice something that wasn't quite right. This extra little window of time helps to cement that feeling of confidence you need if your performance is to be excellent rather than just good. Don't let yourself down by having something go wrong that you could have sorted out if you'd prepared properly.

It's difficult to judge how much information you'll need to prepare if you're given a defined time slot for the event. The general rule is that you're better off with more rather than less. At least this way you won't finish early. I'd rather have the choice of leaving some points out and finishing on time than finishing early because I didn't have enough content. So, an element of your preparation should be determining which points are optional (and can be left out in the event that you're going too slowly) and which are not. Be careful though – you don't want to be leaving out essential points that help to achieve your objective.

Get to the meeting room or venue first. Give yourself as much time as possible to set up. Always build in time for unforeseen occurrences (equipment failure, room change, someone introducing themselves to you beforehand and wanting to chat, etc.).

Where?
Try to make sure the room and equipment layout suits you. You need to be 100 per cent focused on your delivery from the start rather than feeling uncomfortable and distracted because something isn't working or is in the wrong place. I never feel comfortable if I haven't actually seen the room beforehand. This isn't always possible though, so, as a second option, try to find out about it – there may be photographs available, etc.

The same principles apply to a formal presentation, where you might stand at the front, as to a meeting where you're sitting round a table. You need to know the answers to the following questions:

- How big is the room and how many people will it accommodate?
- What projection equipment is available?
- Is there natural daylight?
- How many tables and chairs are available?
- What's the situation regarding refreshments?
- How do you control the lights, the heating or the air conditioning?
- Do you need a security pass to get in and out of the room? (Don't embarrass yourself by getting locked out of the room or office area. I speak from experience!)

Work out where you're going to stand and set the room up so that you can move around it if you need to. You *must* be able to have eye contact with every member of the audience throughout. Excellent speakers never forget this essential rule. Ideally, you should avoid turning your back on the audience too. A handy tip is to imagine you've got an embarrassing stain on the back of your shirt and there's no way you can let the audience see it. So if you're using a flipchart or you need to approach the screen to highlight something, bear this in mind.

You need to know where you will stand and set the room up in such a way that you can move around it if you need to.

You shouldn't be too close to the closest members of the audience (you don't want them craning their necks or feeling uncomfortable) and yet you shouldn't be too far away either – the balance shouldn't be difficult to achieve but you might need to move chairs and tables around to find it. Believe me, it's worth thinking about this beforehand. There's nothing worse than realising too late that someone either can't see your screen, is sitting with a table leg in the way, or just doesn't look comfortable for some other reason.

Confident people control the room. It's very difficult to do this if you haven't prepared it to suit you in advance. Set the room up

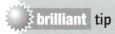
confident people control the room

so that you can take *centre stage*. Don't be a coward … Resist the temptation to set the room up in such a way that the projection screen is the focus of attention. If you look as though you're trying to hide, you'll just draw more attention to yourself.

> **brilliant** tip
>
> Don't forget that you have to be *seen* to be seen to be confident.

Finding the answer to the question 'Where?' is just as applicable to a social event or engagement as it is to a presentation. If you're concerned about meeting new people or people you haven't seen socially for a long time, try to find out how the event is going to be run. Are you going to be sitting down (perhaps at a meal) and talking to one or two people for any length of time? If so, try to find out who they are! That way you can prepare better for the conversation. Or are you going to be mostly standing and mixing with different people? This gives you more flexibility because you can move around as you wish. You'll still need to prepare though – for example, you'll need to prepare for initiating a number of different conversations rather than just the handful that you would if you were sitting down.

What are you going to do?

Having asked yourself the simple 'Why?', 'Who?', 'When?' and 'Where?' questions, you should be in a much stronger position to decide how best to go about your presentation preparation. In other words, how best to achieve your objective.

Try to keep an open mind here. It may well be easier to follow the crowd and do what others before you have done – perhaps use a template presentation that someone else has created or given. Watch out for your gremlin again here. Try to have the self-confidence to think outside the box – think about creating something of your own. You'll find it easier to come across more confidently if *you personally* create the message. You'll know it better and be more familiar with it. It's harder to communicate someone else's ideas confidently than it is your own.

So try to have the self-confidence to do something new, something different perhaps to what others might have done before. Confident people are prepared to accept this kind of challenge. It might involve more work and effort on your part but it's worth it. Having the courage to take a step into the unknown and to try something new will boost your self-confidence. The more you do this, the more confident and comfortable you'll feel. People around you will also start to see you as a more open-minded person who's prepared to try new ideas and to push the boundaries. These are all positive traits that confident people possess.

 **brilliant** example

Nadia

Nadia worked for a children's charity and had recently been promoted to the position of marketing team leader. It was the first time she'd had any real responsibility for people. She now had a small team of five to manage.

Nadia attended one of our confidence-building courses. She was particularly interested in boosting her confidence when speaking in public. This was because she wanted to arrange a weekly meeting with her new team. She ▶

thought this would be a good idea because, in her words, 'the previous head of the team used to do it'.

The 'W' concept helped Nadia to open her mind. Just *thinking* about it made her feel more confident. She realised that having a weekly meeting just 'because the previous head of the team used to do it' was just plain daft! However, she knew that getting her team together on occasions was important because information did need to be communicated and discussed as a group.

So, having considered the 'W' concept she came up with a plan for her new weekly meetings:

 **example**

1   Why? – Meeting objectives:

   ● To ensure that information is communicated to the team on a timely basis.

   ● To provide the team with an opportunity to discuss problems and current issues.

   ● To provide the team with an opportunity to present ideas for more effective working.

2   Who? – Attendees:

   ● Five team members (two inexperienced, three experienced).

   ● Joe (sales manager) to attend on alternate weeks.

3   When? – Date and timings:

   ● 11 am on Monday (not 9 am as before because people always had issues to attend to first thing on a Monday).

   ● Meeting not to last longer than 1 hour (if further issues need discussing, another meeting should be arranged).

4   Where? – Location:

   ● In the Boardroom (not huddled round someone's desk in the office as before, where distractions continually interrupted).

- Allows for use of PowerPoint presentation software with laptop and projector.
- Sends message that meeting is important.

5   What? – What sort of shape will it take?

- Informal but more serious and better managed than previous meetings.
- Request that any issues people want to raise are sent out on previous Friday morning. Agenda sent out in afternoon.
- Meeting split as follows:
  - My part (my personal messages and communication of relevant company information – use PowerPoint when helpful).
  - General discussion of issues others wish to raise.
  - Any other issues or problems.
  - Agreement on actions for the week.

Using the 'W' concept made Nadia realise how bad the previous weekly meetings had been. She'd always felt they were a bit of a waste of time but hadn't really thought seriously about why.

She now had a plan. Prior to thinking properly through the 'W' concept, she'd been very nervous about the meeting – mainly because she felt she lacked the confidence to run it properly. She wanted to start her new role well and felt that this meeting might threaten that.

She now had something concrete to guide her. In fact, once she'd finished her notes using the 'W' concept, she described her feelings: 'It was like having another person there by my side to support me.' The result was that her self-confidence started to rise. This helped her to feel in control right at the start and then throughout her first meeting. This set the precedent for future meetings because she immediately started to generate respect from her team.

brilliant tip

Have the discipline and patience to use the 'W' concept whenever you start your preparation for a pre-arranged event that involves communicating a message to an audience. It lends itself perfectly to preparing what you're going to say at a meeting, a presentation, a job interview or for a social speech.

What ifs

Try to predict the type of questions people might ask you. It's great when someone asks you a question you've already thought about. You'll be able to answer a lot more confidently if this is the case. Put yourself in the place of your audience – ask yourself, 'What would I ask if I were them?'

You might consider using the SWOT principle for this:

● Strengths – what are the strengths of my plan?

● Weaknesses – are there any weaknesses I've decided not to mention?

● Opportunities – what are the wider opportunities that may come from it?

● Threats – what are the threats to its success?

With a little forethought, using the SWOT principle, it's often possible to predict the types of questions you might be asked. That means you can prepare and rehearse some answers to questions that might come your way. Let's say you're presenting the monthly sales figures to your management team. The chances are your report will cover most of the obvious questions the team might have, but what other questions might you predict? What's different about this month? What new questions might be asked? How would you respond? What additional information might you need to have to hand to support more detailed questions?

In particular, spend some time brainstorming the most difficult questions that people might ask, then try to prepare, and if possible rehearse, good answers to them.

Preparation – those final few minutes before the action

You're all set and ready to go. You've covered all the points mentioned above and you're all set to deliver. There's just one essential last piece of preparation to do.

Approach the event as a 'performance' because that's exactly what it is; you're performing in front of others. It doesn't matter if it's a work meeting, a formal presentation, a networking session or a social event; you're still performing.

See yourself as an actor would before going on a stage. You're playing a part too – on your own stage. It involves being your confident self and portraying all the characteristics that confidence requires. You've gone through the W concept; you know what you want to achieve, you've learnt your lines, you've considered the audience, you know what the stage will look like, you know how long the performance will last and you know what the act entails.

BUT, you haven't yet psyched yourself up and 'got into the part'. Ask any professional actor and they'll tell you that focusing your mind on the character you're playing is essential. Remember, the act starts the minute people see you, not when you start talking.

So find a quiet place for a minute or two before you go on stage (in your case, before you walk into the room). This place could be the loo or perhaps an empty room nearby. When you're there, concentrate; visualise yourself walking into the room confidently, smiling with your head up and shoulders back … *Looking the part.*

And then *do it.*

Can you think on your feet?

The reality is that, even if you've prepared well, they'll be some occasions when you're asked a tricky question and you have no choice but to answer there and then.

Self-confidence is key when thinking on your feet. Your confidence will start to build if you follow some of these simple rules:

- *Knowledge* – If you're going to give a reply, make sure you know what you're talking about! That doesn't mean you have to be an expert, you just have to know enough to give a qualified answer. If you're reasonably confident in your knowledge of the subject, that confidence will help you to stay calm and in control even if you unexpectedly find yourself being put on the spot.

- *Never guess the answer* – If you don't know the answer, be honest and say so. Even experts in their field are stumped by a question sometimes. Don't try to make an answer up. There's a good chance you'll get caught out and this could seriously impact on your self-confidence later. Confidently explain that you don't know the answer and make sure you agree a time when you can contact the person subsequently to provide the answer.

- *Try to relax* – It's easy to say but perhaps not so easy to do. At least if you try to relax, you've got a chance. If you don't, you'll look and feel more stressed. You'll have more control of your voice, you'll feel calmer and you'll be able to think more clearly. Taking deep breaths while the person is asking you the question can also really help here.

- *Listen carefully* – Listening properly and attentively requires an effort. Some people forget this. You should be trying as hard when you're listening as you are when you're talking. It's obvious that you'll struggle to think on your feet if you aren't listening properly to the question. Don't interrupt the person – firstly because it's rude and secondly because, if you reply too soon, you may well give a wrong or inappropriate answer.

- *Ask the person to repeat the question* – This gives you those vital few seconds to think about your response. Try to be confident when you do this. Don't let your body language give away the fact that you're unsure of the answer. If your body language is positive and confident, the person will 'read' your request positively, i.e. they'll have the perception that you want to help by making sure you understand the question properly.

- *Repeat the question yourself (out loud)* – This gives you time to think and to clarify exactly what's being asked. Sometimes the person will reply and clarify their question after you've repeated it – that creates even more time for you. If you don't feel that the question is clear, have the confidence to ask for clarification. Again, if you do this confidently, it will be received positively because the person sees that you genuinely want to give a qualified answer.

- *Pause* – Don't be afraid to pause before you answer. People who lack confidence really struggle to cope with silence. They feel exposed and their natural defence is to fill it – normally without thinking about how they're filling it. Then, before they know it, they've said something they wished they hadn't.

- *Use silence* – Confident people can use silence to their advantage. If you think about it, it's totally understandable that you should think about your answer before you give it, so a short silence shouldn't be unusual. If you look comfortable with silence and use it

> confident people can use silence to their advantage

confidently, you'll send the message that you're in control of your thoughts and confident in your ability to answer. Critically, of course, you also create more time to think.

- *Don't waffle* – Once you understand the question clearly, make sure you stick to the point. Your answer should be specific and focused. If you're perceived as a waffler, the person may well start to lose interest – once you see this happening, your self-confidence is going to suffer.

When you've finished giving your answer, resist the temptation to add more information. There may well be a silence after you've finished. Don't make the common mistake of feeling the onus is on you to fill it with more information! You'll lose control of the conversation if your answer starts to drift.

> **brilliant** tip
>
> Don't jump in and give a knee-jerk reaction when someone puts you on the spot. Act calmly and take your time before you answer. There's nothing wrong with saying you don't know, as long as you go back to them with an answer later.

Nerves and anxiety

There will be times when you feel anxious, perhaps even worried about putting some of these principles into practice. That's completely understandable – after all, you're doing things differently to the way you're used to doing them, so they're not going to come naturally.

You're bound to feel a bit edgy about this and as a result you may well get nervous. The key is to try not to see nerves as a negative thing.

try not to see nerves as a negative thing

Believe it or not, nerves are a good thing as long as you can control them! Nerves give you adrenalin; if you can channel it effectively, adrenalin can provide a fantastic boost to your motivation, enthusiasm and confidence. Adrenalin gives you the natural fuel you need to get you into the right gear to tackle the situation. You don't even have to pay for it! Actors and public speakers all feel anxious before they get on the stage (anyone who tells you otherwise is more than likely being economical with the truth). They know how to make this anxiety work in their favour; they know how to channel it to help them enhance their performance.

On the other hand, if you let your nerves get the better of you, you'll get distracted, embarrassed and ultimately your self-confidence takes a nose-dive. The main aim here is to channel your natural anxiety into positive energy that can actually help, not hinder you.

Assertive behaviour – the physical side

When you think about the way you communicate, you tend to think mainly about what you say. That's understandable because your voice is pivotal to sending a message. However, the reality is that only a small percentage of communication involves actual words. Studies conducted in the mid-1960s by Albert Mehrabian, Professor Emeritus of Psychology at the University of California, Los Angeles (UCLA), indicated that the impact of someone's performance is determined 7 per cent by the words used, 38 per cent by the voice quality and 55 per cent by the non-verbal communication used.

You've probably been to work presentations or perhaps social events when you've seen a speaker who is really impressive, a person you would certainly describe as confident. If you're like most people, you thought these positive thoughts about the person and then forgot about them. So, like most people, you missed a trick. The truth is that you *could* have learnt a great deal from that person, but you missed the chance.

When you see someone you would describe as confident, don't just think 'Wow, she's good', think 'Wow she's good, but why?'

The person *must* be doing things to make you form this good impression. But what are those things? Work this out and then model yourself on the results.

 **exercise**

Look and learn

'Example is the school of mankind, and they will learn at no other.'

Edmund Burke, statesman, philosopher and author

The next time you're in a meeting or at a social event, look around the room. Watch how people conduct themselves. Try to set their voice apart from their body language and consider the two separately. Ask yourself who looks confident and who doesn't. Then think about why you've categorised people as confident or lacking confidence. Write down the things people are doing that make them look confident in your eyes. Who looks impressive and who doesn't? Why do some people look more alert than others? Why do you tend to listen to certain people but not others?

Look carefully. You're interested in how they behave – you're looking for the subtle things as well as the more obvious things. Look at how they sit, how they engage people, how they use their body to reinforce their message, what they do with their hands and eyes. You're looking for *anything* that makes them look confident. Very importantly, you're also looking for anything that suggests that they lack confidence.

Reflect now on the list you've made – try to split it between the way they talked and the way they used their body language. The behaviours that support a confident demeanour are just as important to identify as those that don't – you can learn a huge amount by just watching the way other people conduct themselves.

Don't forget – confidence is a skill you can learn. There are many professional sportsmen and sportswomen who will tell you they learnt the majority of their skills by *watching* professionals they admired and then copying them.

The next time you go to a meeting or a social event, reflect on the list you made above before you go in. You might even have it close by during the meeting. Do your best to replicate some of the confident behaviours you've identified in other people. Don't try to achieve them all straight away. Have a plan and focus on one or two each time. Don't move on until you're happy that the ones you've started with are working. This is a great way to boost your confidence – just by making some very subtle changes to your style, you'll be amazed at how people respond more positively to you.

Don't forget also to have the list of negative points you've identified nearby too. These of course are things you *don't* want to be doing. Regularly reflect on this list to make sure you're not slipping into any of those traps.

Finally, make a pact with yourself to never again leave a work meeting or social event without saying something. Prepare beforehand for this by thinking of conversation starters to use at social events or relevant points to raise at work meetings.

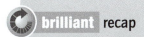 **brilliant** recap

Chapter 6

- Assertive people have influence. Assertiveness is a skill you can learn.
- Truly assertive people have the confidence to both speak up and listen.
- Understand where you are on the assertiveness seesaw: active or passive?

- Say what you think politely and professionally (at work), even when people might disagree with you.

- Preparation is key to coming across with confidence and being assertive.

- Use the 'W' concept as a framework for preparing scheduled events.

- Assertive people have the confidence and courage to say no when appropriate.

- Use anxiety to boost your performance, not hinder it.

- Be vigilant: learn as much as you can from the behaviour of others.

Showing true confidence, verbally and non-verbally

Verbal and non-verbal communication

Having completed the *'Look and learn'* exercise, you've started to consider the concepts of 'verbal behaviour' and 'non-verbal behaviour'. You've probably heard the terms before but have you ever used them constructively in relation to the way *you* come across?

Well, that's exactly what we're going to do here. But first let's clarify what the two terms actually mean:

- Verbal communication = What you say and how you say it.
- Non-verbal communication = What you do and how you do it.

Verbal communication

What are you going to say?

Don't forget to use the 'W' concept if you can make the time. You'll feel a lot more in control when you're working out what you're going to say. In particular, you're using the answers to the 'Why?' and 'Who?' questions – they'll help you to keep focused on your objectives and to have the interests of the person or people you're talking to in your mind at all times.

For situations like interviews, meetings, social speeches and presentations, you might also consider using the mind map process (covered in Chapter 3) – it's a great way of setting out your thoughts quickly and creatively.

Structure

You'll feel more confident and in control if you deliver your message logically. The audience will also feel more comfortable because they'll find it easier to assimilate the information. The secret here is to keep it simple. If you're giving a presentation or a speech, keep it simple by having a clearly defined beginning, middle and end.

Make sure you know what your key points are; if you don't, the audience won't. One easy way to do this is to imagine you've only got one minute on the stage. What would you absolutely have to say to get your point across? What *must* people remember when they walk out of the room?

If you're preparing for a meeting, a well-thought-through agenda will also help.

Credibility

To feel and look confident, you have to feel and sound credible. So what is 'credibility'? A listener sees you as 'credible' when they trust and believe your message. In relation to verbal communication, this means the content of your message must signal preparation, knowledge and relevance. In relation to non-verbal communication it means looking and sounding trustworthy, reliable, aware and in control (we'll come back to how you can help yourself to portray these characteristics later in the chapter).

> to feel and look confident, you have to feel and sound credible

You can blow your credibility very quickly *even if* you look and sound credible. If you promise to do something, make sure you do it – otherwise, the next time you speak to the person, even if you look and sound credible, they won't believe you. This is bound to have negative implications for your relationship with them and eventually your self-confidence will suffer.

brilliant tip

When you're preparing your message, be sure you mean what you say. If you promise to do something, make sure you can and will do it.

Confirmation

We tend to make the assumption that everyone interprets our message the same way. This just isn't true.

How often is it that you tell someone something and they get the wrong end of the stick? Don't worry, it happens to us all. It's not unusual for even the simplest of messages to be misunderstood. It's all down to misinterpretation; the other person has their own interpretation of your message. It's frustrating because, more often than not, the person *does* actually want to help. But, through no fault of their own, they go away with the wrong understanding. This can lead to all sorts of confusion; potentially they'll go away and do something different to what you asked, think something different to what you're thinking or perceive something wrong about your motivations.

You can normally tell by someone's facial expression if they're confused. Confident people don't just see this and accept it, they do something about it. They have the confidence to ask the person what their interpretation of the message is. In other words, they generate a dialogue which ensures *confirmation*.

If you stay aware, you should be able to work out when someone is confused about your message. The difficulty is that, quite often, a person won't tell you – because they're shy, they don't want to look stupid or they don't want to make it look as though they're criticising or questioning you. However, all is not lost if they don't actually verbally tell you they're confused. More often than not, the person will show through their expression that they need help understanding you. The person might not be physically talking and telling you this, but they're still communicating the message to you. Quite often they'll do this subconsciously. A confident person acknowledges this, tries to work out the meaning of the expression and does something about it. Basically, confident people don't have a problem asking if the person seems unsure about their message.

So, reacting to a confused expression is important in order to achieve clarity in interpretation. The real difficulty comes when the person genuinely thinks they have the right interpretation and goes away and does something different to what you were asking. *Don't make the mistake of blaming them straight away for this.* This tends to be what we do – after all, it *must* be their fault if they get the wrong end of the stick! People who think they understand you won't send confused messages through their expression because they're not confused! That's why it's so important to check the message has been received as you want it to be, *regardless* of their expression. This isn't difficult to do – the most difficult part is remembering to do it!

brilliant tip

Don't be too quick off the mark to blame someone for misinterpreting your message. You need to *look at yourself* first. It may be something to do with the way you're delivering the message. It may actually be your fault!

Favourite words

Have you ever listened to someone and wished they'd stop repeating the same word? Words like this tend to fall into two categories: 'filler' words and 'favourite' words.

'Fillers' are words like 'you know' or 'sort of'. They fill the gap (the milliseconds of silence) while the person is thinking about what they're saying. They add nothing to the conversation, are completely unnecessary and can be very distracting and annoying. Some people have a habit of using them all the time. You've probably noticed this on occasions – so don't do it yourself!

'Favourite' words are words like 'obviously' and 'actually'. Some people just can't get out of the habit of repeating these words as they speak. You'll know how distracting this can be too.

The difficulty is that people tend to be completely unaware when they're using 'fillers' or 'favourites'. I've learnt this the hard way myself; I won't forget the time a delegate quietly came up to me after a course and told me I had a habit of saying 'OK' far too much!

The only way you'll know if you're using these words is by asking someone else. Keep a constant eye on this because it's easy to pick up the habit. I regularly ask people if I've fallen into the habit, particularly as I run a lot of courses on my own and don't have a colleague to give me feedback.

Paraverbal communication

To feel confident, be noticed and reduce the chance of misinterpretation, you have to be able to control the *way* you deliver your verbal message. This is sometimes referred to as the 'paraverbal' side of communication. There are huge advantages to be gained from getting this right but there are also significant dangers if you get it wrong. Confident speakers use paraverbal communication to their advantage. This gives them the power to really engage people and control the way they present messages verbally.

You might find it helpful to refer back again to the *'Look and learn'* exercise here. Did you identify any of the following characteristics during the exercise?

Speed of delivery

There is of course the obvious reason for not speaking too fast: people find it hard to assimilate your message and therefore to understand it. You just can't expect people to take it all in if you deliver the message at 100 mph. Watch out here because even if you don't naturally speak fast, if you're nervous, you might find yourself rushing. This is normally for one of two reasons:

● You're desperate to get out of the limelight as soon as humanly possible.

● You're naturally a fast speaker and you're not controlling the habit.

Most people know whether or not they speak fast. Perhaps this was mentioned in the feedback the person gave you when you tried the 'straight talking' exercise (in Chapter 4). If you're still not sure though, try to find out, because it can make a big difference.

Talking too quickly can make you look edgy or stressed. People who look confident just don't do this. They manage to overcome any urge to speed up. They speak at a measured pace that's comfortable for the other person or the audience. This helps them to look and feel in command. It also helps them to control their thought processes. The reason for this is simple – their brain can keep up with them!

> talking too quickly can make you look edgy or stressed

The pause

It might seem like simple advice, but using pauses as you speak is essential to coming across as confident. The difficulty is that a pause means a silence; even the shortest of silences can seem like an eternity when you're in the spotlight. This is one of the reasons why pausing can be so effective – if people are expecting you to say something and yet they see that you look comfortable with the silence, you can use it really effectively. I'm not talking about minutes of silence here, just a second or two.

Be careful though – don't fall into the trap of filling the pause with noise. Noise feels better than silence when people are staring at you … so you say 'umm'. People then start to see you as nervous and lacking confidence.

Most people think the reason your voice sounds juddery when you're nervous is obvious – it's all to do with your mental state. What they don't realise is that actually, in pure physiological terms, nervousness in your voice comes about through physical, not psychological reasons. Therefore, if you think logically about it, if you know what to do, with practice you should be able to overcome saying 'umm' and therefore sounding nervous.

You can't afford to do *anything* that makes you look nervous. If you really think about it, saying 'umm' is just silly – it might make you feel better, but it definitely doesn't make you look better – why do it then?

> you can't afford to do *anything* that makes you look nervous

So how do you stop 'umming'? You'll be relieved to hear that it's really not that difficult; but it does take discipline.

 **brilliant** exercise

No more umms

Find a quiet place on your own. Then, say 'umm' a few times out loud. Now think about what you have to do physically with your breathing to say 'umm'. The answer is simple – you have to breathe out. That means you can't breathe *in* … and that means you're starving yourself of air. It doesn't take long for your voice to be affected by this because all you can do is snatch shallow breaths as you talk. Soon, your voice starts to waver ▶

and break up. It gets worse and worse the longer you speak. The reason is simple – you just don't have enough air in your lungs to be able to project your voice with any strength. It then becomes a snowball effect – you start to hear yourself sounding nervous, you become more and more self-conscious about it and then other nervous traits start to kick in. Eventually your attention is drawn away from what you're saying and you lose control because you're getting hijacked by the state of your nerves.

So, if you want to stop 'umming' there are two essentials to remember:

● Discipline yourself to pause regularly as you speak.

● Make sure you breathe in while you pause.

Just to reinforce that this shouldn't be difficult to do: try saying 'umm' at the same time as breathing in. Have a go now – take a big breath in and say 'umm' while you're doing it. Point made? You can't do it, can you!

brilliant tip

It's essential to pause so that you can breathe regularly while you're speaking. If you don't breathe, you starve your lungs of air. This will severely hinder your chances of projecting your voice confidently.

Not only does pausing ensure you stop saying 'umm'. It also forces you into creating a silence. There are other major advantages too:

● You give yourself more time to think.

● You give yourself a chance to look at your notes and check what you're going to say next.

● You give yourself more time to watch the audience.

● You give the audience more time to take in your message.

● You look and sound in control.

- You give yourself those vital seconds you need to gather yourself when something has distracted you or you've lost your train of thought.
- You give yourself that vital time to breathe.

And of course …

- You look confident – confident people don't have a problem with silence. In fact they use it to their advantage.

Varying the pace

Once you're happy with the speed at which you speak, you can start to think about varying it. If you listen to people who are confidently assertive, you'll hear them varying the pace of their delivery as they speak.

I find that it's really effective if you slow down slightly when you're voicing an important point. If you want to draw particular attention to something, say it slightly slower – you'll see people's heads pop up as you do it. This is simply because you're doing something different – you're varying the pace of your delivery. It's a simple idea but a great technique.

Be careful though – don't overdo it. If you do, your pace will be so varied that it's likely to become a distraction. You could also be in danger of being perceived as patronising if you keep slowing down to make points. This technique is most effective if used sparingly and carefully.

Intonation

You've probably heard people who speak with little or no intonation in their voice; they communicate verbally in a monotonous way. I'd be surprised if you'd describe any of these people as confident. You're probably more likely to use words like 'boring', 'uninterested', 'de-motivated' or 'shy' to describe them. In other words, speaking in a monotone has direct links to people's perception of your confidence.

People with good intonation control the rise and fall of their voice. There are a number of advantages to doing this:

- You sound more interesting.
- You sound and look more interested in your subject.
- You look more relaxed and natural.
- You give a more positive impression.

If you use intonation effectively, you'll also find it easier to emphasise words. This is a great way of improving the clarity of your message. Have look at this sentence and read it to yourself:

I never said she didn't like you.

Now read it again and emphasise the word highlighted each time:

I never said she didn't like *you*.
I never said she didn't like you.
I never said *she* didn't like you.

You can see that the clarity (and even the meaning) of your message can change if you emphasise a different word each time. This could make quite a difference if you're trying to defend yourself against an accusation or if you want to make a specific point.

So, if you tend to speak in a monotone, start trying to modulate your tone. You'll be amazed at how people respond more positively to you. You'll also significantly reduce the chance of them misinterpreting your message.

Enthusiasm

This is infectious. If you sound enthusiastic, there's much more chance that the people or person you're talking to will feel enthusiastic about what you're telling them. It works the other way too of course – if you sound unenthusiastic, it's more likely that your message won't be received positively.

Varying your tone can help with this: people will want to listen to you more if you generate enthusiasm in your voice. Of course, this isn't difficult if you're genuinely enthusiastic about what you're talking about. If so, hopefully you'll naturally sound enthusiastic. I say hopefully because it isn't a foregone conclusion that this will happen. Some people don't sound enthusiastic even when they're talking about something they're genuinely enthusiastic about.

On confidence-building courses, I sometimes ask people to tell us about the most interesting thing they've ever done in their life. It's amazing how some people do this. This is what happened when Scott told us about his *most interesting experience ever.*

 **example**

Scott

Scott told us about an experience he'd had on holiday in South Africa. He'd gone on an organised trip to see great white sharks. He recounted in detail how he'd been lowered from the boat in a cage and how the sharks had circled it. He told us how close they came, how they bumped the cage and even how he could 'see right down into the mouth of one of them past the razor-sharp rows of teeth'. He told us how terrifying it was and how he'd never forget it – ever …

Scott told the whole story in a monotone voice with no emphasis at all. In other words, you would never have thought it was the most interesting thing he'd ever done. It got to the point where you started to wonder if he'd actually even enjoyed it, let alone considered it the most interesting thing he'd ever done.

If you struggle to sound enthusiastic about something you naturally feel enthusiastic about, imagine what's going to happen when you're telling people about something you're not naturally enthusiastic about!

This perhaps might be a situation at work; you might be talking about a work topic that's important but that you don't feel particularly interested in. In situations like that, you've got to make a major effort to pump yourself up so that you come across enthusiastically. If you don't, you'll sound uninterested yourself.

brilliant tip

Enthusiasm is infectious; it can work for you if you project it, but against you if you don't.

Non-verbal communication

There are two themes to consider here:

- Making sure your body language isn't a distraction.
- Using your body language to support and reinforce your message.

Distractions

It's essential that you're aware of any unusual physical habits you have when you communicate. The last thing you want to be doing is distracting the person while you're talking to them. You need to make it as easy as possible for them to take in your message. Just one small unusual habit could cause a distraction.

> confident and truly assertive people have already worked out if they have any distracting habits

Confident and truly assertive people have already worked out if they have any distracting habits. They've also worked out a strategy to overcome them. The 'Straight talking' and 'Self-perception' exercises (in Chapter 4) will have helped you to identify any habits you have. We may have already covered some of them, so you should already be in a stronger position to address them.

Don't forget that it normally takes about 21 days to break a bad habit or to take on a good habit. So don't get complacent if you think you've cracked it after a week or so. Keep going until you're absolutely certain.

Supportive body language

I'd like you to use your imagination for a minute: you're a soldier going into battle. On your belt, easily accessible, you have a number of essential pieces of equipment to keep you alive: ammunition, grenades, bayonet, medical kit, water and radio. At some point, you'll need to use all these items if you're to survive and win.

You can draw a clear comparison here with confidence. Whereas the soldier is going into battle, you are living your life, your confident life. So, on *your* belt you have your own essential pieces of equipment available to support you: eyes, posture, walk, hands and facial expression. Just like the soldier, it's essential that you use all of these physical traits in order to win. Winning for you is looking and feeling confident. We all have our belt with the essential equipment on it. People who lack confidence tend to forget it's there.

So how can you make the most of the equipment on your belt?

Effective eye contact

It's amazing how people's perceptions can differ when they see a person not making eye contact when they're speaking to them. These perceptions do have one thing in common though – they are all negative. Here are some of the comments I get on my confidence-building courses about people who have poor eye contact:

'They don't believe in what they say.'
'They don't know what they're talking about.'
'They look shifty and untrustworthy.'

'They aren't interested in the audience.'
'They look nervous.'
And of course …
'They lack confidence.'

There are some really simple techniques you can use to improve your eye contact.

Have the confidence to take a moment to look at the person or people *just before you speak*. This sends the message that you're not frightened and you're in control. It's a great way of commanding immediate attention. Without even saying anything, you'll also send the message: 'I'm ready and I'm confident'. They'll see this and if there's a hubbub of general conversation going on, they'll soon stop. If possible, don't start talking until there's complete silence.

Confident people make bold eye contact but they don't stare people out. Try to look people in the eye while *they* are speaking. But while *you* are speaking, it's natural to look away on occasions; people expect this while you're thinking about what you're saying.

If you're talking in a small group, try to look at each person regularly. Try to find the balance: you shouldn't hold your eye contact for too long because you'll make the person feel uncomfortable. On the other hand, you do need to hold it for long enough to make 'contact'.

I rarely meet people who are naturally good at this. The majority have to work hard at it to get it right. It's worth it though because, once you've cracked it, you'll see a huge difference in the way people respond to you.

brilliant tip

Good eye contact tells the person you're aware, you care and you're in control.

This exercise should help if you need to improve your eye contact:

 **exercise**

Ghost writer

(This technique works for a group of up to 20 people.)

The next time you're at a meeting, a party or social gathering, or presenting to a group, imagine you have an invisible colleague working with you (I know this sounds daft, but bear with me here). This person is sitting in the corner of the room watching your eye contact. Your colleague has a chart with the name of everyone in the room listed on it. Their job is simple: every time you look at someone while you're speaking, your colleague puts a tick against the person's name to record your eye contact. After the gathering, you sit down with your colleague to analyse the results. Ideally, they show that you gave each person in the room an equal share of your eye contact while you were talking.

There are a number of benefits to this exercise:

- You don't forget to look at people.
- You give each person an equal share of your attention.
- You don't stare at one person throughout. (You may have been on the receiving end of this on occasions and wondered why the person speaking continually looked at you!)
- By looking at people, you engage them and send a clear message that you're interested in them.
- You look confident and in control.

You can't really use this technique for large groups of people. For larger audiences, try looking at them in small groups, picking one person out every now and then. Try to spread your focus across the whole audience so that no one feels left out.

Posture and stance

Some people just look confident. They don't need to do or change anything; they just have something about them. But why is this and what is that 'something'? More often than not it's to do with their posture. The way you hold yourself has a major impact on your body language and conveys your level of self-confidence. You don't need to say anything to give the impression you lack confidence; poor body language can give it away on its own.

 exercise

Mirror image

You'll need a mirror for this exercise, preferably a full-size one so that you can see your whole body. You need to stand in front of it – but, before you do that, make a conscious effort to stand naturally, just as you normally would.

Now look at yourself – have a really good look and ask yourself a simple question: 'Do I look confident?'

If you don't think so or you're not sure, try experimenting a little – try holding your head up, breathe in and push your chest out a little, keep your back straight and push your shoulders back.

Your aim is to look relaxed and yet aware and proud. I find that positioning one foot slightly in front of the other makes a difference, particularly when standing in front of or within a group. The alternative is to 'plant' yourself with both feet on the same line. This doesn't look so natural. Always make sure you have a small gap between your feet; you'll look rather stiff and tense otherwise. Try to distribute 40 per cent of your weight through your heels and 60 per cent throughout the ball of your foot and your toes. This brings your body position slightly forward and helps you to look more alert.

As long as you don't march up and down, there's nothing wrong with moving a little as you talk. It'll help you to look more relaxed. It should also help you to engage all members of the audience; moving your body (even just your upper body) to face people when you look at them, perhaps when asking or answering a question, helps to create a stronger link with them.

These simple changes in posture will help you to look and feel more sure of yourself.

They also help you to look more prominent. The reason for this is simple – having an open posture automatically takes up more space. It sends a physical message that you're not afraid. It also stops you looking defensive or shy.

Your walk

Have you ever thought about the way you walk? It seems like an odd question, doesn't it! It's worth thinking about though because, just like posture, it can have an impact on confidence. It's absolutely true that if you walk confidently, you'll feel more confident.

> if you walk confidently, you'll feel more confident

There are some simple things to consider to make this happen.

Don't walk too fast or too slowly; try to find the balance. Too fast could make you look in a panic or as though you're rushing, perhaps out of control. Too slowly could make you look de-motivated, uninterested, hesitant and could of course make you late! People with an air of confidence about them walk at a measured pace. So, reflect on the pace you walk at and try changing it if you need to. You'll need to think consciously about this; walking is such a natural action, we rarely think about how we do it. Try to incorporate the tips about posture while you're improving your walk – posture and walking should work together.

Your hands

Some people think that the best thing to do with your hands is to keep them by your side or hide them because otherwise they'll be a distraction. *This is madness.* It's akin to the soldier going into battle without using the ammunition on his belt.

Your hands should be an essential support to your verbal message. If used well, they can help you to reinforce your point. When in a relaxed environment, people tend to use their hands naturally to clarify and support their message. However, when in the spotlight, some people either completely forget about or lose control of their hands.

Don't fall into the trap of thinking your hands will distract people. I very rarely meet people who are too demonstrative with their hand movements. The vast majority of people don't use their hands enough. The trick is to try to relax; let your hands do what comes naturally. The natural action is for them to move in support of your verbal message. This is why confident people look relaxed – their hands move naturally and in a coordinated way with their voice.

> confident people look relaxed – their hands move naturally

The following tips should help:

- Use your hands to emphasise or clarify your point. For example, if you plan to address a number of points, use your fingers to support this: hold up one finger when you're referring to point 1, two fingers for point 2 and so on. You could use two hands for this if you prefer – rest the fingers of one hand on the outstretched palm of the other. Another example might be when you're describing a minor issue – lift your hand so it can be seen, and bring your forefinger and thumb together to emphasise how small the issue is. There are of course many other examples that could be given. Try practising on your own using your hands to reinforce your verbal message. It can make a huge difference to people's perception of you.

- Have a 'default' or resting position for your hands when you're not using them. Otherwise, you'll look as though you don't know what to do with them. I find the most comfortable resting position to be arms slightly bent in front of your body, with your hands held together and fingers gently interlocked (without whites of knuckles showing!) You might prefer a different resting position so try experimenting and find your own – it's important that you're comfortable and relaxed with it, otherwise you won't use it.

- Use calm, smooth and flowing hand movements.

Here are some of the 'don'ts' to watch out for when using your hands:

- Don't use fast or jerky hand movements – they don't portray a confident demeanour and can be a distraction.

- Don't point at people.

- Don't fold your arms (unless in an informal environment where it doesn't matter). This could be seen as defensive and might make you appear unapproachable.

- Don't tap on surfaces with your fingers.

- Don't fidget, wring your hands or touch your face or neck. This can suggest you're feeling nervous or insecure; just as children often scratch their leg when telling a lie, adults scratch the back of their head, rub their arm or fiddle with their fingers when they're nervous.

- Don't forget that some hand signs can be deemed as inappropriate or rude in some cultures.

Facial expressions

Your facial expressions can convey a whole host of messages to people about your emotions, your feelings, your confidence levels and your interpretation of their message. Some people are naturally very expressive and open in their communication style. Others tend to be less expressive and more 'private' and don't give much away at all. My experience is that confident people tend to fall mostly into the 'expressive' category although this is not always the case.

If you see yourself in the 'less expressive' category, try to think about how you could benefit by being slightly more expressive. For example, how often do you smile when talking to people? If the answer is 'not much' or 'never', you're missing a trick. If you really want to project confidence, try to smile more. A smile makes a huge difference. It makes you feel and look more confident and it makes the other person feel more at ease. A smile can send so many positive messages in an instant: happiness, awareness, interest, friendliness, approachability, sensitivity, enthusiasm and of course ... confidence.

> a smile can send so many positive messages in an instant

 **brilliant** exercise

Guess who

Picture this – you're in a room with a group of people. You're either sitting round a table or standing. Any minute now, someone is going to open the door and come into the room. This person has a few seconds to look at everyone in the room and guess who's in charge. Your aim is simple – to make sure the person picks you. There is one constraint only for the people in the room – *no one is allowed to talk.*

So, what are you going to do? The answer is simple because you haven't got much choice – you use your body language to win. You need to get your posture right, regardless of whether you're sitting or standing. In order to be picked, you'll need to look like the most alert and confident person in the room. If you're standing, the tips we've covered on your posture and stance will help.

To be picked as being in charge while you're sitting could be slightly more of a challenge because you only have the top half of your body to work with.

The temptation while you're sitting is to sit back, perhaps even slump in your chair. Try to resist this – you need to look aware, enthusiastic and interested the whole time.

These actions should help:

- Sit leaning slightly forward in your chair.
- Keep your back straight, your shoulders back and your head up.
- Make sure you can see everyone and make regular eye contact with each person.
- Keep your hands above, not below the table (when you're not using them to support your message, rest them on the table).
- Use your facial expressions to help you to look alert and aware.
- Smile when appropriate.

Try this exercise the next time you're in a meeting or with a group of people in a room. It's a great way of helping yourself to look and feel more confident.

Space

You'll feel more confident if you feel comfortable with the 'space' around you. You probably know how uncomfortable you can feel if someone is too close to you during a conversation. Sometimes it's referred to as 'invading your personal space'. The perception and use of space differs significantly across cultures, so it's worth doing some research if you work or socialise within a culture with which you aren't familiar.

Don't make the mistake of thinking that to be confident is to be close enough so that you can control people's personal space. This is counter-productive because it just makes them feel uncomfortable. Ideally, you need to find the balance between proximity and distance.

Most of the time, you should be able to control the space around you. For example, you can make simple adjustments to where you position yourself to make sure you're not too close to people when you're in a group. Don't forget the 'Where?' element of the 'W' concept: if you have advance warning, it's sensible to prepare the room if you're running a meeting or giving a presentation.

Space isn't just about the physical space around you though. It's also about your appearance. You'll feel more confident if you're happy with the way you look. Taking the time to do a little preparation can help here too. For example, if you know the dress code beforehand, you won't feel over- or under-dressed. Perhaps revamping your wardrobe or getting a haircut might help. There's one major rule here regardless – never look a 'mess'. The word 'mess' doesn't only relate to your clothing, it also relates to your personal organisation and time management. If you look rushed, disorganised, ill-prepared or scatty, you're making life much more difficult for yourself if you want to feel confident.

Sometimes people don't realise how significant the messages you give out through bad use of space can be. For example, if at work your desk is always disorganised and in a mess, you send out negative messages. If you then, during the course of your work, need to be assertive and influential, you'll tend to be on the back foot. Your colleagues will see you as a 'messy person'; this could even have an impact on the respect they have for you. If this is the case, you're just making life more difficult for yourself.

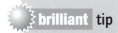

brilliant tip

Take the initiative and control your personal space. Dress appropriately, keep tidy and use the space effectively.

First impressions

It takes just a very quick glance for someone to evaluate you and form a judgement when you meet them for the first time. Without even thinking consciously about it, the person forms an opinion about you. In literally just one second they're basing this on your body language, your appearance and your demeanour.

This first impression can be nearly impossible to reverse or undo. That's why it's so important to get it right. The last thing you want to be doing when you meet someone is to give away any sign that you lack confidence. Any negative impression you give will set the tone for the relationship that follows.

> a first impression can be nearly impossible to reverse or undo

So, regardless of whether it's in your work career or your social life, giving the best possible first impression is vital.

More often than not you'll have prior warning before you meet someone new. That means you'll have time to prepare. You don't need hours for this, you don't even need minutes – just a few seconds will do as long as you know how to make the most of the time you've got.

In short, your sole focus during that window of time before you shake the person's hand should be on looking confident. To do this you need to employ all the traits that constitute assertive behaviour. You should by now know what you need to work on here. Start this straight away the next time you meet someone new.

Remembering names

I don't know about you but I'm always impressed by people who remember names. These people pretty well always fall into the group of people I'd describe as being confident. It's impressive if you meet someone and they then address you by your name; it's even more impressive if they do this when you're one of a group of people they've just met.

Remembering names is a simple concept that can really help you to stand out and be seen as a confident person. People seem to think it's much more difficult to do than it actually is; you'll have heard people say 'I'm hopeless at remembering names' – maybe you're one of these people yourself!

The main reason why people struggle to remember someone's name is that they don't register it in the first place. When you meet someone for the first time your senses are drawn mainly towards what they look like and how they behave. Without realising it, you get distracted from what they actually say. Of course, one of the first things they'll say is their name – and that's where the problem lies. You can't forget their name because you never actually heard it in the first place.

There are some simple steps you can take to get better at remembering names:

- *Prepare* – Get into the habit of accepting that an essential element of introducing yourself is hearing and remembering the person's name.
- *Ask* – If the person doesn't tell you their name, ask politely what it is.
- *Clarify* – If you don't hear the name clearly, politely ask them to tell you it again.
- *Associate* – Link the name with something physical that distinguishes the person.

- *Repeat* – Say the name to yourself until you remember it without thinking.

- *Write* – If it's a group, write their names down in the order they're sitting. Then test yourself with each person's name until you're comfortable you know them all 'off pat'.

- *Use* – Now that you've done the hard work of remembering the names, *use* them. Address people by their name regularly. They'll notice this, and their perception of you as a confident, aware and assertive person will build.

It's completely normal to feel a little anxious or nervous when you meet someone for the first time. Think consciously from now on about how you introduce yourself to people. By using positive verbal and non-verbal behaviour, you'll be able to give the very best first impression. The more you do this, the more confident and comfortable you'll feel when meeting people. When the other person sees that you are at ease, they too will feel more relaxed and the conversation is likely to flow much more easily.

 **brilliant** recap

Chapter 7

- Communicate a confident message; control what you say and how you say it.

- Be physically impressive; control what you do and how you do it.

- Be credible and confirm your message is being interpreted correctly.

- Reinforce your message; get the 'paraverbal' right.

- Is your body language distracting? Find out and, if necessary, do something about it.

▶

- Practise using all the physical attributes you have to come across confidently.

- Enthusiasm is infectious; make sure others catch it from you.

- Control your personal space and use it effectively.

- Give the very best first impression and remember the name!

Confidence at home and at work

et's just reflect for a moment on the reality. You're three-quarters of the way through *Brilliant Self Confidence*; you're getting to the point where your Self-Confidence Project is going to really get into gear. There are still some significant issues we haven't yet touched on though. There are two key questions you need to answer:

1 Do you feel satisfied with the way your life is going?

2 How motivated are you?

Finding the right balance

It's difficult to feel satisfied and happy if you don't have a balance to your life. I find that confident people often feel content and happy because they're in control of their lives. They've found the happy medium between the four key elements in their life:

● Their commitments and time spent at work

● Their love for and time spent with their family

● Their personal health and fitness

● Their time spent on 'personal' recreation and hobbies.

There's a direct link here to self-confidence. Most confident people have found an acceptable balance between their responsibility to others and their own wants and needs. This helps them to feel satisfied and to stay positive. We notice this about them at work and socially because it's reflected in their behaviour, their approach to life and the way they conduct themselves.

Importantly, they also tend to be *realists* – they've come to terms with the fact that we all have responsibilities. For example, the majority of people have to work to earn a living. Most confident people accept this and get on with it.

You'll struggle to stay confident if you don't feel in control and satisfied with your life. Why? ... because you'll end up demotivated, rudderless and, ultimately, failing while others achieve.

A lot of people who lack self-confidence feel it's selfish to think of themselves. This is just not true; confident people realise that balancing your own wants, needs and aspirations with your responsibility to others is vital.

 **brilliant** exercise

Life balance

Even if, on the face of it, you feel satisfied in your life – try this exercise. Ask yourself if the balance in your life is right. Be realistic though – for example: don't kid yourself that you aren't happy because you spend more time at work than you do on holiday!

It's important that you open your mind and think creatively when you do this, particularly when you're thinking about yourself and the things you'd like to do or achieve. Some people find it helpful to refer to the strategic objectives and tactical goals they set (in Chapter 3) when they're doing this exercise. Look at these again and satisfy yourself that the time and effort you're planning to put into different aspects of your life are balanced fairly.

The 'life balance' exercise is about the present though. It's about the way you're leading your life at the moment and whether or not you've got your priorities right. Try thinking about how much time you spend at work and then consider the other aspects of your life which are or *should be* important to you. This is a personal and private exercise and only you will know what's important to you. It might help to think in terms of:

● Your responsibility to others (work, family etc.)

● Your responsibility to yourself (work, enjoyment, health, hobbies etc.).

Some people find it helpful to actually map out how much time they spend on the different elements of their life. This highlights any inconsistencies and shows whether or not you're spending too much time on one particular aspect of your life. In other words, whether or not you've got your priorities right.

Have a look at this pie chart put together by Ailsa. She's calculated the amount of time she spends on different aspects of her life over a weekly period.

Ailsa has chosen family, health, work and recreation as her key elements. You can see straight away just by looking at the larger, white portion that she spends a lot of her time at work (this includes her journey to work).

Ailsa is married with two young children; she works full time and sometimes doesn't get home until after they've had their bedtime story (read by her husband, who works part time). The main message she's learnt from doing this exercise is that she just doesn't spend enough time with her children. So this simple exercise led her to change her work pattern to accommodate … an exercise well worth doing!

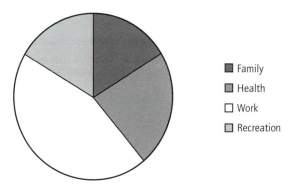

Figure 8.1 Life balance

Have a go at developing your own pie chart; you could choose the same elements as Ailsa or you might decide to change them to reflect your own life more specifically. For example, if you spend a lot of time cleaning the house, then cleaning could be one of the elements you include on the chart. Include anything you think takes up a significant amount of time. Don't forget to put sleeping time on the chart. Ailsa decided to include sleep in the health portion (and realised that she probably doesn't get enough of it!).

Remember, you're looking at a period of a week in your life. It needs to be a fairly 'typical' week so don't choose a week that doesn't reflect the general pattern of your routine. Make sure you include the weekend so the exercise reflects seven days' worth of your time. Some people find it helpful to break the week into days and then to break each 24-hour period down.

Ultimately, your pie chart represents 168 hours of your life. Once you've allocated times to activities, you should have a good feel for how your time is spent. When you've finished the chart, reflect on it and ask yourself if you've got your priorities right. The pie chart can be a real eye opener. In fact I've known some people who've radically changed the way they live, simply as a result of what they've discovered by doing this exercise.

Personal effectiveness and discipline

People's perception of how you come across to them socially and at work isn't just based on how you look and sound. It's also based on how you behave and how you organise yourself. You'll feel more confident, and there's more chance people will perceive you as confident and in control, if they see you as an organised, tidy and efficient person.

Personal organisation

How many confident people do you know who are disorganised? If you can think of any at all, they tend to be the exception to the rule. Confident people are usually organised, both practically and mentally. There's a lot of truth in the saying 'disorganised desk, disorganised mind'.

> confident people are usually organised, both practically and mentally

If you tend to be disorganised in the way you run your life, you'll struggle to think clearly and logically. If you can't think clearly and logically, you'll let both yourself and others around you down. The result, of course, is that nothing people perceive in you is positive. At best they'll see you as messy and scatty; at worst they'll see you as lazy, unreliable, unprofessional, selfish … and the list goes on.

The difficulty is that people won't necessarily tell you they see you like this, they'll just perceive it. More often than not, if they perceive it, you'll detect it in their behaviour towards you. As we've seen already, this could have a significant impact on your work and personal life.

So, when you started thinking about building your self-confidence, you might not have seen the link between personal organisation and confidence. Don't worry though, you wouldn't have been the first person not to. The key now is to address the issue if you need to.

Managing your time

Being efficient and organised with the use of your time is essential. If you feel that your life is under control and that you're making the most of it, your sense of well-being will be stronger. This is bound to help with your personal self-belief in relation to what you would like to achieve.

Try asking yourself how you tend to approach life. Are you what is often referred to in 'time management language' as a Type A personality or a Type B personality?

- *Type A* – Describes people who like to get things done and push themselves quite hard. They'll cram a lot into their day. However, they sometimes take on too much and fail to set aside enough time for relaxation or reflection on where they are going.

- *Type B* – Describes people who work at a slower pace and are able to bring a healthy balance to their lives. They aren't so conscious of time deadlines. People who demonstrate extreme Type B behaviour often let others down because of their laid-back nature.

Having established where you see yourself on the Time Line (see Figure 8.2), consider whether or not you would benefit by changing your approach slightly. You might find that you fall between Type A and Type B behaviour. That's not unusual. In fact, it's quite a nice place to be because you're not leaning towards either extreme.

Don't be late!

Type A people tend to be late because they've got so many other things to do. Type B people may be late because they're just more relaxed about the concept of time. There are the obvious reasons for not being late, the main one being that you'll let others down and waste their time. Some people naturally feel bad when they let people down, others don't. Ask yourself where you stand here.

So, what's this got to do with confidence? Put simply, if you want to feel confident at all times, you'll need to have this considerate mentality built into your mindset.

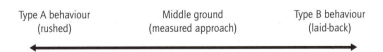

Type A behaviour   Middle ground   Type B behaviour
   (rushed)   (measured approach)   (laid-back)

Figure 8.2 The time line

Letting people down is a good enough reason on its own for not being late, but there are other more personal reasons that can also have a direct impact on your confidence:

- If you're late, you're already on the back foot. The other person already sees something negative in you because you've let them down. You can't afford to project any negativity at all if you want to come across, and therefore feel, confident. If you're late, you'll have a slope to climb, created completely through your own making, rather than a level playing field.

- If you're late, you'll cause a distraction for yourself (and others). You'll be thinking about what people think of you rather than how you're coming across. You know you're late and this will be (or certainly *should* be) on your mind. You can't afford any distractions if you're trying to come across confidently. You need 100 per cent attention on the task at hand – i.e. to look and sound confident.

Wherever you find yourself on the Time Line, make the decision right now that you will endeavour never to be late again. Of course, if you're delayed by events outside your control, then that's understandable. Don't forget to explain this though when you get there!

brilliant tip

Don't be late, don't even be on time – be slightly early. Then you've got time to prepare yourself to come across confidently. You'll be on the front foot (and already one step ahead of people who haven't yet arrived).

Staying healthy and keeping fit

'Life is like riding a bicycle. To keep your balance you must keep moving.'

Albert Einstein

I'm not sure that Einstein meant this quote to be taken literally – after all, it's unlikely he was a fitness fanatic! More than likely, he was referring to keeping active in terms of new ideas and thinking so you don't get left behind. But perhaps there is a more literal meaning to this quote ... Let's presume so for the moment.

If you're out of shape, there's more chance you'll feel insecure and unattractive. So by keeping in reasonable shape, you'll improve your physical appearance and feel more energetic.

Of course, this doesn't happen on its own. You'll need to make the effort to achieve it. It's true that there's a direct link between your physical state and your mental state. The healthier you are, the more energy you'll have. The more energy you have, the easier you'll find it to maintain a positive mental attitude.

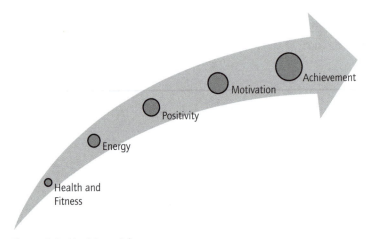

Figure 8.3 Health and fitness

It's also been proven that physical exercise is a powerful natural antidote to depression. So there are no negatives about keeping fit, there are only positives.

Consider health and fitness on two levels:

- Your general health
- Your physical fitness

General health

With the exception of illnesses over which you have no control, everyone should be able to stay healthy. If you're sensible with your diet and keep it balanced, if you ensure your body isn't physically stressed, if you get enough sleep and you get exercise, then you should be able to stay in good general health. If one of these key requirements is missing due to your lifestyle, you should think about making a change – you'll struggle to stay positive otherwise.

Physical fitness

It's also important to keep physically fit. Don't worry though, you don't have to be super-fit – you just need to keep your body in trim. This is harder for some people than others due to physique and dietary considerations. BUT – everyone can do it. It just takes self-discipline. You need to find a realistic level of fitness that suits *you*.

This is worth trying if you haven't tried it already. Of course, 'physical fitness' means different things to different people. Don't worry about other people – don't try to match others unless you feel it would help. Manage your expectations here and do what *you* feel comfortable with. For one person this could mean walking twenty minutes a day, for another it could mean running for twenty minutes a day.

There are all sorts of fitness regimes you could consider – too many to list here. Do some research on the internet and pick one that suits you. You might also consider joining a gym, perhaps even joining a club. It doesn't have to be a running club – it could be any type of sport or perhaps a walking club. Start off slowly and work up, don't challenge yourself too much at the beginning.

Finding your focus

Understanding what drives you

To feel confident and in control of your life, you need to know what drives you; you need to know what makes you tick. Knowing what you actually *need* to keep you enthusiastic about life is an essential component of personal motivation. Knowing what you *need* is much more important than just knowing what you *want*. Needs are essential requirements, wants are desirables. There's a significant difference here in relation to feeling and being confident.

Put simply – if you don't get what you want, you'll probably feel sorry for yourself and perhaps frustrated. That's not great but it isn't the end of the world – you should still be able to overcome this with self-discipline. However, if you don't get what you *need*, you'll come to a grinding halt.

Personal motivators

Opposite is a list of ten aspects of life that people feel are important to them. Look through them and think about them in terms of what you *need* in life, not so much in terms of what you *want*. Most people know themselves well enough to be able to differentiate between the two. Then rank each aspect of life in terms of its importance to you; mark the most important as 1 through to the least important, 10. If you want to discuss your answers with someone else, don't do this until you've completed it, otherwise they might distract you from your personal thoughts.

_____ Enjoyment

_____ Interesting work

_____ Religion

_____ Salary

_____ Personal development and learning

_____ Recognition and appreciation

_____ Job security

_____ Family

_____ Ambition

_____ Friends and relationships

Each individual is different; understanding which of these aspects of life are most important to you personally is essential. Knowing this will help you to get your true priorities in order. You'll have a clearer focus and you'll be able to shape your life to accommodate it. If you don't know what drives you and keeps you motivated, you can't aspire to it and you can't provide it. If you can't provide it, you'll end up in a downward spiral. It's impossible to maintain a positive mindset if you're not getting what you need in life to keep you enthusiastic and motivated.

Most people have a rough idea of where their orientation tends to be. Be careful though, don't make any presumptions – you might be surprised to find that, deep down, you need something different to what you originally thought; therefore it could be that you're not getting it – simply because you didn't know you needed it. Your mental attitude will suffer if this happens.

When you reflect on the list, consider it in the light of the most important motivators you've identified as being the things you need and the less important being the things you want (or perhaps even don't want in some cases). Focus on the motivators at the top of your list – they're the things that *really* matter to you; the things you *really* need. Now ask yourself if you're getting them. If not, why not and what do you need to do to change?

It's just as bad to feed yourself constantly with something you *don't* actually need. That would be like putting unleaded petrol in a diesel engine. Yes, you're re-fuelling the car but watch out, you'll cause some serious damage; ultimately your engine seizes and you break down. It's also a huge waste of time and effort – time you could have spent filling up with the right fuel and getting to where you want to go.

brilliant tip

To feel confident, it really helps if you feel motivated and positive about life. To feel motivated, you need to know what makes you tick.

Handling conflict with confidence

One common denominator between self-confidence at home and at work is interpersonal conflict. Conflict is a natural phenomenon. You can reduce the chance of it happening but you're never going to get rid of it completely. So, it happens. If dealt with calmly, it can in fact be a positive thing.

It can help you to:

- clear the air
- clarify what the other person is thinking
- put your point of view across
- discover a better way of doing something.

It doesn't matter if you're having an argument at home with a friend or member of your family or you're having a disagreement at work with your boss or a colleague: the same rules apply to dealing with conflict.

There's an art to dealing confidently with conflict. Just as an army needs a strategy to win a battle, so, on a more tactical level, do *you* need tactics to deal with a personal skirmish. We all encounter these skirmishes from time to time, some of us even on a daily basis. But how do you normally react? You'll probably tend to react in the same way each time; that's because you have your own instinctive way of dealing with conflict.

If you've started to use some of the tips covered so far in *Brilliant Self Confidence*, you should find that the number of conflict situations you encounter has started to reduce. For example, the simple act of adapting your communication style should make a huge difference to your relationships at work, at home and socially.

Your instinct

Have you ever thought constructively about how you instinctively react when someone criticises you, says you're wrong, frustrates you or winds you up? Some people come out of their corner fighting every time, even when they think or even know the other person is right. Other people will just give in or avoid the conflict, even when they know the other person is wrong. What do you tend to do?

The conflict zone chart (Figure 8.4) shows two conflict handling extremes. Some people will 'contest' regardless of the situation; others will just 'give in'. Look at the chart and put a cross on the line between 'contest' and 'give in' to show where you think your instinctive approach to conflict falls.

So you've drawn a cross somewhere on the line. Most people assess themselves correctly in terms of their leaning but some people find it difficult to judge the degree to which they lean; in other words, the strength of their style. To help with this, go to **www. thinkconfidence.com** and complete the Think Confidence Conflict Style Questionnaire. It's a simple questionnaire that

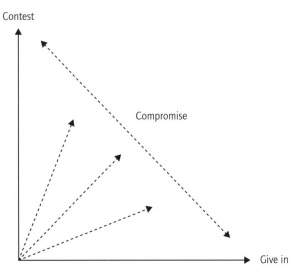

Figure 8.4 The conflict zone

helps you to identify your instinctive conflict style and the degree to which you use it.

Some people score themselves at one or the other of the extremes; others see themselves falling in the middle. This middle ground is the area of 'compromise'. You might think that to compromise is the right approach regardless of the situation; the solution that suits both people. Well that's true, but not *all* the time.

You might also think that to be at one or the other extreme is wrong; after all, to 'give in' can't ever be right, can it? Well yes, in certain situations, it can. Equally, at the other extreme, some think that to 'contest' an issue strongly and to insist you're right could be construed as 'over-doing it'. Try not to think like this either; as long as you aren't aggressive or violent, contesting an issue can also be right in certain situations. The key is to have the self-discipline and confidence to choose the right approach for the right situation.

 **example**

Rob

Rob was organising a weekend trip to France with a group of five friends. They'd arranged to meet in the local pub one evening. The aim was to discuss and agree where they'd stay, how many nights they'd stay for and what the travel arrangements would be. Everyone had agreed that Rob would be the best person to coordinate the trip because he'd been to France the year before on a similar trip with other friends. Rob was happy to be in charge.

The meeting started off well. They were all good friends and had known each other for some time. There was, however, one person in the group who was more outspoken than the rest and throughout the evening tended to dominate the conversation. Rob found this odd because during the course of the evening it transpired that this person (Lynda) had never even been to France before!

Rob remembered from his trip the year before that they'd really regretted not hiring a car for the weekend. They'd decided to go on the ferry as foot passengers and get the train to the village they were staying in. This had turned out to be a big mistake because, although beautiful and picturesque, the village was in the middle of nowhere. As a result, they'd ended up having to get taxis everywhere and this had meant they'd ended up spending much more than they'd planned. Not having a hire car also meant they'd had no flexibility – every time they wanted to go out, they had to ring for a taxi. This turned out to be really frustrating.

So, Rob explained all this when they were talking about transport arrangements. Lynda, however, just would not listen. She was adamant that the cost of taxis would be less than hiring cars. However, Rob had already worked out that, even if they hired two cars, it would still be cheaper than hiring taxis throughout the weekend and, of course, they'd have the flexibility to go where they wanted when they wanted.

This led to a disagreement. Rob began to feel very uncomfortable with the situation because he just didn't like arguing. He ended up giving in to ▶

Lynda even though he knew he was right. None of his other friends in the group could make up their minds what was best. One or two of them even tended to side with Lynda because she was so direct with her views. Rob just didn't stand up for himself so they weren't convinced by his argument – even though he'd actually been there and experienced the problem!

Rob just wasn't a person who felt comfortable contesting an issue. His instinct was to give in whenever he found himself in a conflict situation. He felt particularly uncomfortable with Lynda because she was a person who would instinctively contest.

The whole group lost out eventually because they didn't hire cars and, just as Rob had predicted, they regretted it.

brilliant tip

When you think you're right, don't give in. It's time to be actively assertive in order to contest the issue. You'll need to motivate yourself to do this, particularly if your instinct is to give in. Make a pact with yourself not to let this happen the next time you think you're right and the other person contests.

Like Rob, the majority of the people I meet who lack confidence tend to either give in or do their best to avoid the conflict in the hope that it will go away and not come back. The trouble is, the problem rarely does go away; more often than not it will fester and then come back with a vengeance.

So, you're probably getting a feel for what I'm suggesting here. People who have confidence and use this confidence in a balanced manner are able to deal with each conflict situation that confronts them in the way that best suits. They have the self-control and sensitivity to avoid or perhaps even give in when they should and they have the self-belief and self-confidence to stand up for themselves when they think they're right.

Identifying the type of conflict situation you're encountering is the first step to making a judgement and doing something about it.

So, if any of the following applies, you need to dig deep, present your case confidently and *contest* the issue:

● When you're sure you're right and the potential repercussions of the other person winning the argument are serious.

● When you're sure you're right and any delay in presenting your case could have a negative impact.

 **example**

Mike

Mike was on a skiing holiday in Austria with his family. An easygoing, confident person, Mike would only contest an issue if he really felt he was right or that a matter of principle was involved.

He'd hired a snowboard for his son Toby to use. Unfortunately, at lunchtime on the last day of their holiday, one of the boot straps (bindings) on the snowboard broke while Toby was using it. As a result, Toby couldn't ski on the last afternoon and Mike had to take him back to their apartment using the lift system up and down the mountain. This took all afternoon because they were a long way away and had to use a number of different lifts to get back. They'd wasted a whole afternoon of their holiday.

Mike was certain that Toby wasn't responsible for breaking the snowboard and that the hire shop should take responsibility because it was a 'mechanical' failure rather than a 'breakage'.

So, when they arrived back at the shop, Mike calmly explained what had happened to the shop owner. He also explained that neither he nor Toby   ▶

had been able to ski since lunchtime, they'd wasted the ski passes they'd paid for and they'd had a long trip back using the lift system.

Mike made it clear to the shop owner that he didn't feel it was fair for him to pay for the hire of the snowboard for the last day … And that was when the conflict started because the owner completely disagreed. Mike stood his ground even though the owner became quite annoyed … 'If you hire a car and have an accident, you pay for it … hiring a snowboard is just the same,' he kept on saying. But Mike wouldn't budge because as far as he was concerned he was right. He retorted, 'If I hired a car and I had an accident which was my fault I would have to pay for it, but if I hired a car and it broke down through no fault of my own, I would not … you have hired me a snowboard and the binding has snapped – my son did not break it.'

And so the argument went on, but Mike stood up for himself because he thoroughly believed he was right. As a result the owner backed down and didn't charge him for the last day's hire of the snowboard.

So what's the moral of the story? If you feel strongly about something, prepare before you speak and have facts and reason to back up your argument. Mike prepared before he went back to the shop. He took a deep breath before he went in and presented the owner with his case. It worked.

On the other hand, when might it make sense to *give in*?

- When you know the person is right or has a better idea than you.

- When you know *you* are right but the issue is of such minor importance that it's just not worth getting into an argument.

- When you're working with someone who's learning (perhaps a young person) and you don't want to demotivate them. The person is full of energy and enthusiasm and wants to help. They come up with an idea that you know won't work because you perhaps tried it when *you* were learning. As long as the consequences of them trying their idea and failing aren't likely to be serious, let the person have a go. They'll feel more inclined to come up with ideas in the future because they know you'll listen. If you don't let them have a go, you could end up with a demotivated person who doesn't think you value their opinion or, perhaps even, trust them.

Or perhaps, it would be more sensible to avoid the conflict (this isn't giving in; you're just avoiding the conflict for the moment with a view to addressing it again later if it's still there).

So, when would it make sense to *avoid it*?

- When tempers are getting frayed and people aren't thinking straight.
- When the issue is of such minor importance that it's just a waste of time to argue about it.
- When you're not prepared properly with your argument.
- When you're not in the right frame of mind.
- When you're in a place that isn't appropriate (perhaps a public place where others can overhear you).

There are times too when the most sensible course of action is to *compromise*. If you score yourself between the two extremes on the Conflict Zone chart, your instinct will tend to push you towards the middle ground of compromise.

The compromise style lends itself best to the following situations:

- When a solution is moderately important but not worth the effort or possible continued conflict that might result from either contesting or giving in.
- When you need to achieve a temporary settlement to a larger issue.
- When you're under time pressure.

- When both sides have essential needs to consider.
- When you're dealing with someone of equal power or authority.

Choosing the right style

Be aware of your instinctive way of dealing with conflict; it could be to contest, to compromise or even to give in. Whichever it is, don't worry; there's nothing wrong with any of these approaches. Be aware though: you'll react to conflict in your natural instinctive way time and time again if you don't consciously think about it. The key is to make sure you don't 'default' into your comfort zone when your instinctive approach isn't the *right* approach.

brilliant tip

Pinch yourself next time you face conflict. Look at how you're behaving. Ask yourself if you've chosen the right style. Prepare yourself if you need to switch from your natural style.

Showing emotion

There's nothing wrong with showing your emotion! In fact, you'll find it hard to deal with conflict effectively if you withhold your true feelings.

More often than not, the main reason we hold back is that we fear the consequences of showing our emotions. We worry that we'll embarrass ourselves and we wonder what the person will think of us and how they might react. It's for this reason that people tend to show and share their emotion more readily at home than they might at work.

Try to set aside these worries (particularly at work). After all, there shouldn't be any embarrassment if you control the way you communicate your emotion. Some people might even see your lack of visible emotion as a sign that you don't care ... not a good way for your work colleagues to perceive you.

Continually holding in your emotion can be like blowing up a balloon – breath by breath it gets bigger until, eventually, unless you release some of the air – BANG! Releasing *some* of the air is the important thing to remember here. If you let go of the balloon and release *all* of the air, it'll fly away wildly and you'll lose control. So, controlling the way you release the pressure is the key to communicating your emotion effectively.

These essential rules should stand you in good stead:

● Think carefully before you talk or act.

● Communicate your emotions in a controlled way.

● Don't let your emotions cloud your judgement.

● Make sure you're receptive to the emotions of the other person.

● Adapt your communication style to accommodate the style of the other person.

brilliant tip

It's more damaging to bottle up your emotion than to share it. Just make sure you prepare yourself and communicate it with self-control.

Dealing with difficult people

Even when you have the confidence to change the way you approach a conflict situation, from time to time you'll still encounter people who you find it difficult to deal with. Some of these people will be people you already know. That means you can pre-empt and prepare for what's going to happen before you see them; it's unlikely they're going to change the way they behave.

The first thing to do when dealing with a person you find difficult is to reflect on your natural communication style. Simply adapting your style to match theirs may well be enough to convert a 'difficult person' into a person you don't feel uncomfortable with. Hopefully you'll have nipped the problem in the bud before it's even started.

So, what should you do if you've tried adapting your style and still the person is being difficult and insisting they're right? Here are some ideas:

Stand up for yourself

I've mentioned that a lot of the people I meet who lack confidence find the hardest conflict situations to be the ones where they have to stand up for themselves. This may mean 'contesting' an issue, insisting on your rights or strongly voicing your concerns. They find this hardest because it's against their nature. If you're one of these people, you're going to find this one of the most challenging parts of your Self-Confidence Project.

You'll find that being more assertive will help here. Think back (to Chapter 6): if you tend to lean naturally towards the passive side of the Assertiveness Seesaw, you'll have to work hard to fight your gremlin. Extreme passiveness normally means giving in. Your gremlin will be trying hard to keep you on the passive side of the bar. You'll never be able to stand up for yourself if you stay there. Remember the *Brilliant Self Confidence* principle – *don't let the gremlin get you.*

The three simple steps in Figure 8.5 should also help when you need to stand up for yourself and when you're dealing with difficult people at home or at work.

Figure 8.5 Dealing with difficult people

Step 1 – *Suss out the situation*

If the person wants to speak, let them; be quiet and don't rush in; control yourself and wait it out. Let them get it off their chest. Don't interrupt them. Actively listen, look alert and don't get distracted. Control your body language – don't let your body speak for you instead of your mouth. Don't fidget, shrug your shoulders, use submissive facial expressions or body language. All of these traits signal that you lack self-confidence and could make you look apologetic. Just stand or sit still, face the person and look them in the eye while they're talking.

Keep the person and the problem separate. No matter how much their behaviour frustrates you and winds you up, try to keep an open mind. The person might not just be being difficult, they might actually have a valid and good point.

When they've finished, try to hold the silence. This might put them off their guard. They're expecting you to say something – so you've got the initiative now. Make sure that when your chance to respond comes, you insist that nobody interrupts you. This shouldn't be a problem if you had the self-control not to interrupt *them*. If you're interrupted, politely remind the person that you deserve to be heard – it's your turn now.

Step 2 – *Deliver*

Make sure you know what you want to achieve and the basis of your argument. If you don't, you're not ready – so find more time to prepare. If *you* don't know, how can the other person be expected to understand your point of view?

Take control by setting out the facts. There's no harm in repeating the other person's argument or position back to them. This way they'll know you've listened. Having heard it again, they might even realise how stupid or weak it sounds! Repeating it back to them also gives you more chance to think about it.

Then, speak authoritatively in the first person. This means saying 'I' more than you might normally. For example, it's more constructive to say 'I don't agree with you' than 'you're wrong'. There's nothing wrong with saying 'I disagree' or 'I feel strongly that that is the wrong approach ...'. Make sure you have some substance to back up your opinion though. Otherwise the other person could counter that you're basing your opinion simply on judgement, not fact. This could also mean that you start to lose credibility – and then you're on the slippery slope to losing the argument.

There's one exception to the principle of saying 'I' – never say 'I'm sorry' for putting forward your opinion. Never apologise for standing up for yourself unless, on reflection, your behaviour was aggressive or inappropriate in some way.

Speak assertively; try not to stutter and don't mumble. Remember to breathe! This will help you to think and speak at a measured pace. Be positive at all times and don't be frightened to encourage discussion about the issue; even though the person might eventually realise you're right, they won't necessarily accept this if they don't feel you've given them a chance to present their thoughts in full.

Step 3 – *Take the initiative at the end*
Take control of the conflict situation by being the one to conclude it. Have the moral courage to offer an ultimatum if you think it's warranted. Try to end it on your terms but be prepared to compromise if you judge it to be fair and necessary. If you've decided to contest the issue, never walk away without either solving it or agreeing a next step.

 **brilliant** example

Naomi

Naomi was rather like Rob in her approach to dealing with difficult people. Her instinct was to give in rather than hurt someone's feelings or, even better, to avoid the conflict altogether in the hope that it would go away.

The trouble was, she'd tried both these approaches and still she kept coming into conflict with a particular person (Marie). They were both managers of a call centre team dealing with holiday insurance. They worked different shifts and as a result didn't see much of each other.

Naomi had got to the point where she felt the team was suffering due to Marie's insistence on shaping the way it operated. Naomi would regularly come in to work and find that Marie had introduced a new procedure that she knew nothing about. Not only did Naomi feel this was unprofessional because they were supposed to be managing the team jointly, she also felt that some of these new procedures were wrong and inefficient.

Naomi decided to try out the three-step plan to deal with Marie. She had to summon up a significant amount of courage to do this because it meant going completely against her instinct. The first thing she did was arrange a meeting with Marie. She explained beforehand that the reason for the meeting was to talk about the most recent new procedure Marie had introduced.

Step 1 was easy for Naomi – all she had to do was look Marie in the eye, listen and take in exactly what she said. She didn't even have to invite Marie to speak because she immediately launched into justifying why she'd introduced the new procedure. Naomi also made a point of taking some notes while Marie was speaking. They were just far enough away from each other so that Marie couldn't read them. Naomi noticed her looking down at them every now and then. This made her feel more confident; she was sure she detected a sense of unease in Marie's behaviour.

Step 2 was harder – Naomi had to deliver her points; this was against her natural inclinations. She waited until Marie had finished. She finished the note she was taking and looked up. She let the silence extend. Just as she sensed Marie was about to start talking again, she spoke up. She started by summarising what Marie had said (her notes were helpful here). She explained clearly why she felt the procedure wasn't working and suggested another solution. At one point Marie tried to interrupt. Naomi said very ▶

assertively, 'I've listened carefully to your points – I would like to finish explaining mine please.' Marie stopped talking immediately.

Naomi didn't let Marie interrupt until she'd finished. They then had a discussion. Naomi was clear in her mind right from the start that she wouldn't give in. She'd thoroughly researched her argument and was prepared to stand up for it. She was surprised to see that after a while, Marie backed down and, believe it or not, *accepted* it.

Step 3 went well too – Naomi kept the initiative by explaining she didn't feel it was in the best interests of the team for Marie to make decisions without involving her. She proposed that from now on they meet once a week so that they could manage the team more effectively together. Marie seemed a little wary of this idea but agreed to it in the interests of the team.

Naomi found that subsequently, over time, her working relationship with Marie improved. It was never fantastic but the change in her approach to dealing with the conflict with Marie made a huge difference. Marie started to get used to this and in time even admitted privately that she respected Naomi more for it and found it easier to work with her because she 'knew where she stood with her'.

These tips should also help you to stop conflict escalating when you encounter it:

- Ask yourself whether it really matters that much – in other words, is it worth getting into an argument. What's the worst case scenario?
- Change the subject – stop talking about it.
- Don't repeat it to others to make you feel better or just to get it off your chest.
- Put yourself in the other person's shoes – see it from their side.
- Choose not to associate with negative people or people who argue for argument's sake.

- Focus on fact, not emotion.

- Clear your mind. Get out of the environment, go for a walk or do some physical exercise.

- Compliment the person. Some people are very susceptible; you might find that just being nice can help you to win the argument or get your way.

- Acknowledge that you've heard the other person's point of view. Some people just need to know that you're listening and you understand their concerns.

- Use open-ended, not closed questions. An open-ended question invites discussion, a closed question invites a yes or no answer. For example:

  - Open-ended question – 'How did you think that meeting went?'

  - Closed question – 'Did you think that meeting went well?'

- Manage the person's expectations; don't promise you can do everything. If you say you'll do something, make sure you can and will do it. You'll gain more respect and people will know where they stand with you.

- Email – don't send emotionally charged or angry emails. Try to deal with the issue face to face. If you have no choice and must reply to someone by email, try writing the email first but not sending it. Have a break and cool down, then have another look at it. Don't send it until it is written in a controlled and professional way. It could backfire on you otherwise.

- Sleep on it – it's amazing how a night's sleep can put a different perspective on a disagreement.

Have no fear!

There should be no need for you to fear conflict at home or at work from now on. You'll feel more confident to deal with disagreement if you try to see it as something that's bound to happen from time to time – you might not be able to stop it happening but you *can* deal with it. Approach it as a natural phenomenon that's part of life. It's a fact that people behave and think differently and therefore, on occasions, they'll disagree with each other.

That's actually a good and positive thing – if we were all the same, we would progress as a race of people at a much slower rate. It's proven, for instance, that the most successful teams are the ones with the most diverse mix of personalities, knowledge and intelligence. The key to real success is understanding how to turn any differences of opinion (conflict) into agreement and effective action.

If you really think about it and try to analyse why conflict occurs, more often than not you'll come to the conclusion that it stems from differences in personal style and approach. A disagreement may start as a result of differences in opinion but the escalation to conflict often comes as a result of differences in behaviour and personal style. In extreme cases the differences in opinion are completely forgotten and the clashes in style and behaviour take over as the core conflict issue itself.

brilliant tip

Expect disagreements to happen. Your challenge is to deal calmly with each situation so that it doesn't escalate to conflict. Remember the three key steps: Wait, Deliver, Take the initiative.

Are you just plain shy?

Another common denominator between confidence at home and at work is shyness.

A lot of the people I meet on confidence-building courses describe themselves as 'shy'. They struggle to come forward to speak both at home and at work. Overcoming shyness isn't difficult but it does require discipline, preparation and courage. In other words, it requires a number of the tips and behaviours already mentioned in the book. Put these into effect and you'll find it easier to deal with your tendency to feel shy.

'You gain strength, experience and confidence through every experience where you really stop to look fear in the face. You must do the thing you cannot do.'

Eleanor Roosevelt

 **example**

Jenny

Jenny had two young children at primary school. Being shy, she found it hard to talk to the other mums at the school gate. It got to the stage where, at pick-up time at the end of the school day, she'd find herself hiding in her car watching all the other parents chatting in the playground waiting for the kids to come out.

The situation got worse and worse; as the other parents got to know each other better, she knew no one. It got so bad that she ended up getting out of her car as the kids came out, picking them up, talking to no one and driving home. This went on for a whole year! Of course, the longer she didn't talk to people, the harder it became to strike up a conversation.

It wasn't until her seven-year-old daughter Daisy asked her why she never talked to any of her friends' parents that she realised she had to do something about it.

So she booked a confidence course and that's how I met her.

After the course she had a plan which she put into practice straight away. It required discipline, preparation and courage.

▶

1. Discipline

Firstly, Jenny vowed to herself that never again would she sit in her car waiting for the children. She would force herself to talk to at least one person every day at the school gate. Ideally, each day she would choose a different person so that she started to get to know people more quickly.

2. Preparation

Secondly, she prepared. She worked out what she was going to say while she was on her way to the school in the car. The things she thought of revolved around topics she'd have in common with other parents – for example, school clubs, sporting events, etc. She also prepared in her *mind*. In other words, she psyched herself up. This was probably the most important part of her preparation because it was mainly her *fear* of talking to the other parents that was holding her back. Lastly she prepared by visualising herself actually doing it confidently. By the time she got to the school she was ready.

3. Courage

Thirdly, she acted. When she arrived at the school, she looked at the parents waiting at the gate and decided on the person she would talk to. She had the topics at the forefront of her mind.

She courageously and confidently got out of her car, walked to the gate with her shoulders back and head up and went through with it. The first day it was a major challenge just walking up to the person (Jenny even described it as 'embarrassing'). The second day, it became a little easier, the third day even easier. By the end of the first week she'd struck up a conversation with five different parents. The next week, one of the parents even came up to *her* for a chat! And on it went.

Of course, introducing herself to other parents wasn't just good for *her*, it benefited her children too; they saw their mum behaving more 'normally' and it opened up more opportunities for them to go round to their friends' houses to play. Even better, they got invited to more birthday parties!

Jenny overcame her fear of talking to other parents in the play-ground. The same principles apply whenever you have a fear of doing something: you'll need discipline, preparation and courage.

So, the time has come to show your confident self …

Make an immediate difference At Work:

- Speak up more in meetings, never leave without contributing.
- Offer to do that presentation, don't wait to be asked.
- Show an active interest in others; get yourself round the office more.
- Hold yourself confidently; use charismatic body language around the workplace.
- Be assertive; say what you're thinking when you've got a point to make.
- Liven up; show some energy and a degree of urgency to get things done.
- Be decisive; stand up and be counted.

Make an immediate difference At Home:

- Widen your circle of friends; socialise with positive, not negative people.
- Be active; keep healthy and fit.
- Get your priorities right; make sure you have a balance between work and recreation.
- Get motivated; ensure you're getting what you need.
- Enjoy life; do something for yourself every now and then.
- Achieve more; set personal objectives.
- Don't hide; take the initiative at social events.

Approach this in simple terms. Use the GARMS principle (Figure 8.6). It's self-explanatory. It works.

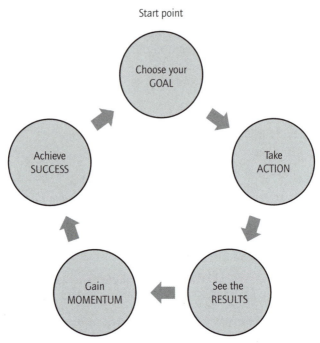

Figure 8.6 The GARMS principle

 **brilliant** recap

Chapter 8

- Consider the four key elements to life and find the right balance.

- It matters if you're messy and disorganised; it can have a negative impact on how people see you.

- Help yourself to stay confident by keeping healthy and fit.

- Personal motivation and drive are essential to keeping a confident frame of mind.

- Know your natural conflict style. What's your 'default' position when under pressure?

- Have the courage to use the right style for the right conflict situation.
- Decide on a plan for dealing with difficult people.
- If you're shy, adopt DPC: discipline, preparation, courage.

PART 4

Keeping up the momentum

Dealing with setbacks

Wouldn't it be fantastic if from now on it was all plain sailing? You'd wake up every morning feeling confident, ready to take on the world and win. Plus, you'd see me as a genius for writing a miracle book! ... But that's the point; it would be a miracle, unfortunately.

You don't need me to tell you that it's not going to be like that. Yes, there'll be some days when your self-confidence is high and you'll feel good, but other days will be more challenging. That's the reality so it's best not to kid yourself.

Ideally, of course, you'll have more good days than bad days! There's no doubt that as you learn to be more confident, the bad days will diminish. But they'll still be there on occasions because you'll have setbacks along the way. Setbacks are normal; they happen, even confident people have them. Sometimes the cause of these setbacks will be of your own making; other times, something will happen that you couldn't have predicted.

The key is to approach setbacks positively. Don't get down about them. They're bound to happen. In fact, there could be a lot you can gain from them. If you think negatively about them, you've got no chance of seeing this. Don't forget the Indian proverb, '*I complained that I had no shoes, until I met a man who had no feet.*'

Picture this:
You before you started your Self-Confidence Project:

Figure 9.1 Adrift

Your Self-Confidence Project is going to give you a framework to use, or, as in Figure 9.2, the navigational equipment you'll need in your boat. But it's not going to be all plain sailing. It never is.

So how do you cope with setbacks?

During my service with the Armed Forces, I had the opportunity to spend a week submerged at sea on a naval exercise in one of the Royal Navy's Nuclear Submarines, HMS *Tireless*. The exercise involved testing the crew on how they dealt with emergency procedures when under attack. It was all about 'damage control'.

There's an interesting analogy here. There are a number of parallels between how the crew reacted when under pressure and how you'll need to react when your confidence levels are

You during your Self-Confidence Project:

Figure 9.2 En route

being tested. For them the submarine was damaged, for you it's your self-confidence. How did the crew deal with the problem? Simple, they initiated *damage control procedures*; and that's exactly what you'll need to do.

Putting damage control into action

'Damage control' only works if you're organised, disciplined and calm. This is impossible to achieve when you're under pressure if you don't have a plan of action that you're familiar with. Depending on the problem, the submarine crew would know automatically which plan to activate. They'd practise these procedures relentlessly so that when the situation occurred for real, damage control would work.

So what can you learn from this approach? ... A lot.

When something goes wrong or not according to plan, you can be pretty certain that your confidence levels will dip. It's at these times that you'll need the self-discipline to activate your own damage control procedure.

Here's a proven process that you could use (Figure 9.3). The more you practise it, the more natural and instinctive it will feel.

Phase 1: Don't panic

Panicking will get you nowhere, in fact it'll probably make things worse.

Things didn't work out the way you planned: the presentation didn't go well, the meeting was a failure, you didn't get the interview, you didn't quite have the confidence to introduce yourself at the party, you couldn't fill that awful silence, someone else got the promotion you hoped for, your performance appraisal didn't go well … Don't panic! It happens! It's normal. Even confident people have setbacks.

So, take a few deep breaths and accept the fact that things don't always go according to plan.

Phase 2: Think rationally

It may seem like the world is caving in around you, but it isn't. So try to get the setback in proportion. Don't fall into the trap of building it up to be something it just isn't. Try to think rationally about the situation. Rather than getting upset and emotional, stop what you're doing and reflect on what's happened. Try to

Figure 9.3 Damage control

be objective. Think logically, set aside the emotion and, if you're feeling embarrassed about what's happened, try to set this aside too so that it doesn't affect your thought processes.

Ask yourself if your setback is really that significant. You have control over this: it'll be as significant as you make it in your mind. Ask yourself what the implications of the failure are. What's suffered as a result? Really think about this because, if you think logically without being swayed by emotion, you'll probably find that the implications aren't anything like as bad as you thought. They rarely are.

By now you should be coming to terms with the setback. Now it's time to work out what you can learn from it and how you can stop it happening again. You don't have to be perfect; after all, nobody else is. Don't lay blame; take personal responsibility and ask yourself what you can do to get back on track.

Phase 3: Assess the problem

The word 'crisis' originates from the Greek, meaning 'a moment to decide'. This didn't come about by accident.

So, let's say a work presentation hasn't gone well. Now you need to work out why. Be specific: it's not enough to just think 'I didn't come across very well' or 'People weren't interested'. What you need to be asking yourself is 'WHY' didn't you come across very well and 'WHY' weren't people interested? Ask yourself why and you'll give yourself something tangible, something that you can actually act on to stop the setback happening again.

Perhaps you've worked out that people didn't listen to you because you didn't seem very enthusiastic, but *why* didn't you seem enthusiastic; what gave them this impression? Once you've thought logically about it, perhaps you've worked out that it was … because you didn't *sound* enthusiastic … why didn't you *sound* enthusiastic ... because you *spoke too quickly* and your voice sounded *monotonous*. GREAT! ... now you've thought it through logically, you've got something concrete to improve on.

Phase 4: Take action

Decide what needs to be done to address the situation. Is there any immediate fall-out from the failure? If so, do you need to act quickly or do you have time on your side?

If you've decided you need to act quickly, be careful, don't make the situation worse with a knee-jerk reaction. It's always worth reflecting before you act, even when it seems you haven't got the time. Even a few seconds will help.

In most cases, you won't need to act immediately (even though your heart says you should) so take stock and decide what you need to do to stop the setback happening again.

You've established that the presentation didn't go well because you spoke too fast and sounded monotonous. So you know what you've got to work on. Now you've got to be disciplined and *seek out opportunities* to improve. Don't wait for another presentation to come along: it could be weeks or months.

Be proactive, have the confidence to think positively about how you could *create* opportunities to practise. It doesn't have to be a presentation; any situation that requires you to speak in front of a group will do. Work or social meetings are a great example. Next time these come up, prepare yourself beforehand and practise speaking more slowly and in a more engaging way. For example, modulate the pitch of your voice. Practise, practise, practise and you'll start to see results.

And of course, don't let your gremlin get you. He'll try to convince you to hide when a chance to practise comes because he wants you to fail. He thrives on failure.

Phase 5: Review the situation

Keep track of how you're getting on. If the setback involved a specific situation or event, you MUST challenge yourself to replicate it so that you know you can actually do it better. It's fine to practise using similar situations but at some point (sooner rather than later) you must put yourself in the same situation as the actual setback itself.

So, if it was a work presentation you struggled with, you'll need to challenge yourself to give another work presentation. Without this you'll never have the peace of mind to know that you can actually do it well. Your self-confidence simply won't improve.

> ### brilliant tip
>
> Confidence comes from the knowledge that you can succeed in situations where previously you failed.

Initiating damage control should be easier if you think positively about the process. A new study carried out at the University of Kent, UK found that 'positive reframing' is an effective way of dealing with small daily setbacks. Positive reframing means simply looking at a minor failure or setback in a different light.

It works well for the small setbacks we all experience that don't actually matter but seem embarrassing or important at the time: for example, the stupid mistake you hadn't noticed on the email before you sent it, the flippant comment you made but immediately regretted, the embarrassing silence, the time you spoke just as someone else decided to … All these setbacks are so minor that they don't warrant worrying about. So don't let them bother you or knock your confidence.

Try looking at them in a more positive light. Try laughing to yourself about them! Yes, laughing! The study found that people who laugh to themselves about life's daily small setbacks actually feel more satisfied at the end of the day. And of course, their self-confidence remains intact.

In essence, positive reframing means looking for something good in what happened. So, coping with these minor setbacks can be a lot easier if you try to see the positive aspects of what you're describing as a failure. For example, it's a lot more productive to focus on what's been achieved rather than on what's not been achieved.

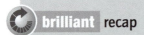 **brilliant** tip

Don't ruminate about small failures and drag yourself further down ... try to accept what happened, look for positive aspects and, if it's a minor event, have a laugh about it.

brilliant recap

Chapter 9

- Setbacks are a reality of life. Even very confident people have to deal with them.

- How you overcome them will be crucial to maintaining momentum in your Self-Confidence Project.

- View each setback as a positive learning experience, not a failure.

- Put 'damage control' into action: stay calm, be rational, assess the situation, take action, review.

Using your new-found self-confidence to really change your life

Embracing the change

'It's not the strongest who survive, nor the most intelligent, but the ones most adaptable to change.'

Charles Darwin

You've probably already realised that putting your Self-Confidence Project into action is going to mean making some changes in the way you think and behave. You may have made some changes already. You may even have done some things you previously *could not do*. If so, brilliant! You haven't let the thought of doing something different hinder you.

Some people do find the concept of change harder to deal with than others. Don't worry if you're one of these people; no one finds it easy. There's a simple reason for this: human nature instils within us a natural and instinctive caution whenever we're faced with doing something new or different. This of course is a positive trait: it stops us rushing into things that are ill-conceived, foolish or even dangerous.

People with self-confidence are able to control this natural caution. They understand why it's there but they have the self-confidence and self-belief to make sure it doesn't work against them or hold them back when they need to change their behaviour or when an opportunity arises.

So how do you find the right balance between caution and action? In other words, how can you help yourself to get moving with the changes *you* have decided to make as part of your Self-Confidence Project? To do this, you need to understand what happens in your mind when you're faced with the need to change.

Dealing with change within your Self-Confidence Project

You may well be wondering what I actually mean by 'change'. In terms of your Self-Confidence Project, 'change' means doing any of the following *differently* to the way you normally do them:

- *Communicating verbally* – For example: one of the changes you may have decided to make is to speak louder or perhaps more slowly in certain situations.

- *Communicating non-verbally* – You may have identified that you need to look people more in the eye when you're talking to them or perhaps you need to change your posture.

- *Thinking* – Perhaps you've realised that you tend to be too negative and that you need to think more positively from now on.

- *Behaving* – You may have realised that your present lifestyle isn't conducive to being more confident. For example, you may have decided that you need to get a grip of yourself, be more organised and more focused.

These are just a few examples of changes people decide to make. The changes *you* need to make for your Self-Confidence Project to be successful may be similar or perhaps very different. You'll have got a good feel for these during the perception exercises (in Chapter 4).

A natural reaction

It's natural for you to feel more safe and secure if you carry on doing what you used to do rather than try out something new. This is because we tend to prefer to do what we know works, even if it doesn't work very well! This may also be true of your approach to 'change' in relation to your Self-Confidence Project; you'll probably feel more uncomfortable moving out of your comfort zone (the way you used to be) than you would if you just stay as you are.

The critical point to have at the forefront of your mind though is that through *Brilliant Self Confidence*, you've made some rational decisions; you've decided that certain things *aren't* working for you. These are the things that are hindering your confidence levels, self-belief and possibly even self-esteem too. Therefore, they *must change* if you want your Self-Confidence Project to succeed.

Try to keep this in proportion though; for a lot of the time, there's no problem with staying as you are. It's just in certain situations and with certain people that you need to change the way you communicate and behave.

The change process

'Man cannot discover new oceans unless he has the courage to lose sight of the shore.'

André Gide

Coming to terms with the need to make these changes involves your mind going through a number of stages (don't worry; I'm not going to boggle you with some complicated psychological theory here). It's true though that we all go through the same thought processes when dealing with change.

In simple terms, there are two stages to this:

- *Stage 1* – Coming to terms with and accepting the need to change.
- *Stage 2* – Putting the change into practice.

Although we all go through these two stages, some people move more quickly than others. That's simply because, depending on their personality, some people accept and embrace change more willingly than others. There's a difference of course between thinking of and initiating the change *yourself* and being told or invited to change by *someone else*. Most people find the latter more challenging; not only do you have to make the change, you also have to come to terms with the other person's reasoning. In the main, your Self-Confidence Project involves the former which, you'll be glad to hear, tends to be easier; *you* are the initiator of the change and, therefore, it's yourself you need to reason with and convince of the need. This surely shouldn't be a problem – should it?

Hopefully, you're already well into this process. Ideally, you will already have come to terms with and accepted the need to change; what you've read so far in *Brilliant Self Confidence* should certainly have whetted your appetite. Let's not make any assumptions though – like I said, some people move through the process more quickly than others, so it's helpful to look at what's going on in your mind in a little more detail.

Stage 1 - Coming to terms with and accepting the need to change

Denial

To succeed at your Self-Confidence Project and change for the better, you'll need to break some pretty strong moulds. Regardless of whether you initiate it yourself or someone else suggests it, the very first thought that comes into our minds when the need to change is introduced is *denial*. We deny the need for it and don't want to do it. For some people, this is just a momentary thought, for others it dwells and then festers; in the worst case, it can be so destructive that it actually stops any possibility of the change taking place.

Without wanting to frighten you, unless you can control it, denial could be responsible for bringing your Self-Confidence Project to a grinding halt before it's even properly started.

Resistance

But don't worry, the fact that you started reading *Brilliant Self Confidence* in the first place suggests that you're already well past the denial stage in terms of accepting the need and wanting to be a more confident person. If so, you've moved on to the next step of the change process – Resistance.

Resistance involves a passive acceptance that you need to do some things differently. Whereas before, in denial, the door of your Self-Confidence Project may have been firmly shut and locked, now, at the resistance stage, you have the key in your hand. You still need to put it in the lock and open the door though. Here are some of the reasons why people struggle to use the key; in other words, why people find it hard to overcome this passive resistance to making a change.

Can you remember ever experiencing thoughts like these? (you'd be unusual if you can't):

- You fear doing it.
- You fear the result of it.
- You can't be bothered to do it.
- You haven't got the time to do it.
- You're scared of taking a step into the unknown.
- You see the need to change as a criticism of you.
- You fear the embarrassment of doing it or being seen doing it.
- You fear the possibility of failure.

You know yourself better than anyone. To get your Self-Confidence Project off to the best possible start and to keep it moving, it's important that you know where you stand here. In other words, how willingly do you embrace change? This exercise should help you to work it out.

 **brilliant** exercise

Think change

Try to think back to times in the past when you've had to make changes. Think of your life as a whole. To help you, here are some examples of changes other people remember in their lives: giving up smoking, getting fit, changing jobs, redecorating the house, being more sociable, etc. These are just some examples, none of which may be relevant to you – but which changes can *you* remember?

Once you've recalled them, think carefully about how you approached them. Try to think right back to the very beginning of each experience. Try to remember how you felt when you first thought about making the change. How long did it take you to come to terms with it? Do you remember denying initially and then resisting the need for it? If so, did you have the self-confidence to overcome this denial and resistance yourself or did someone else have to help you?

If someone else had to help you, you're not alone; you're one of many people I meet who struggle right at the very beginning at the denial stage. You now know from this experience that you'll have to work extra hard at the beginning of your Self-Confidence Project to get it moving. Some people find it helpful to work with a 'buddy' at this stage of the Project. So, if you think you might need some help to get motivated at the start, think of someone (a buddy) who could support you and work with you on it. If you worked with someone during the 'Straight talking' perception exercise (in Chapter 4), maybe the same person could help you and give you some moral support here.

On the other hand, like some people, you might not want any help. That's fine too; after all, your Self-Confidence Project is something personal, something you may well want to keep to yourself. Don't worry if you're thinking like this – as they say, 'fore-warned is fore-armed'. The important thing is that you know from reflecting back on your reaction to change in the past that you're vulnerable to denial and resistance; so now you're in a stronger position to deal with that weakness yourself.

But deal with it you MUST.

brilliant tip

A word of warning: don't allow your Self-Confidence Project to stall before it's really started. Smother your gremlin if it tries to tempt you into denial or resistance. Try asking yourself what the alternative to making the change is; what will the consequences be if you don't change? This alone should be enough to convince you of the need.

Stage 2 – Putting the changes into practice

Exploration

When you reach the 'Exploration' stage in your state of mind, you'll have accepted the need to change and you'll be exploring new ways of behaving and communicating. You're looking to the future, not dwelling on the past. While you're reading this, you might think you've reached 'Exploration' already – if so, that's great! The fact that you're reading *Brilliant Self Confidence* certainly suggests this because you're using the text to *explore* ways of building your confidence.

Don't worry if you feel you're not quite there yet though; it's normal to move back and forth between Resistance and

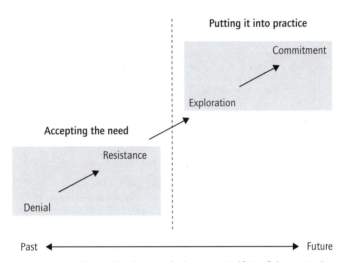

Figure 10.1 Dealing with change during your Self-Confidence Project

Exploration for a little while (see Figure 10.1). It's entirely under-standable that you're a little anxious about some of the things you're going to need to do to get your Project really moving.

So, it's important to work out where you personally are in your mindset right now. If you want to change but your gremlin is still nibbling away at you, you've got a little bit more work to do to silence it. You'll need self-discipline for this.

You'll know when you've truly reached the 'Exploration' stage. It will be like waking up to a new dawn. Denial and Resistance can be like experiencing a tempestuous storm at sea, Exploration is like waking up the next morning to find clear blue skies and calm all around. You can see clearly out ahead, right to the distant horizon. You now need to set your course; without that you're in danger of drifting, going round in circles or, potentially, even heading back the way you came. You can't let that happen.

So during 'Exploration' you're getting your bearings and working out a plan of action. You're clarifying your vision of what you want your new future to look like. You're thinking positively about the real changes you need to make in your life to feel more confident. You're starting to think in terms of the benefits of doing these things rather than how hard they will be to do. You'll probably still feel anxious about doing some of them but the difference is that, whereas before you weren't convinced it was possible to feel and be more confident, now you're starting to believe it really is.

If I were to guess where you are now in your mindset, I'd like to think that you're on the cusp between Exploration and Commitment.

Commitment

Exploration will lead naturally to 'Commitment' as long as you stay positive in your mindset. Commitment is the last stage of the change process. You've set aside any negative thoughts, you've come to terms with what's ahead and you can see the benefits of committing yourself to the changes you've decided to make.

You've accepted the challenge and decided that the effort will be worth it. You feel *committed* to making the Project work. In short – you're all systems GO!

Don't get too carried away though. It's great to be committed but dangerous if you bite off more than you can chew to start with. It's important to manage your expectations and take one step at a time. The objective and goal-setting principles (in Chapter 3) should help you here. Start slowly with small changes so that you don't frighten yourself off. While you are doing this, try to set specific milestones to mark your progress.

True commitment comes with time; it helps if, step by step, you can actually see positive results from your efforts. Slowly but surely your self-confidence will build and your commitment to try new ways of behaving will strengthen.

brilliant tip

People go at different speeds through the change process. It's OK to go slowly as long as you keep moving and don't get stuck. It's also OK to go fast, as long as you truly commit to the change at the end. Don't kid yourself. Commitment means actually doing things differently, breaking some habits and putting yourself in situations that perhaps terrified you previously.

Planning for action

To keep the momentum moving from this point on, you need a plan. The best way to do this is to plan your Project on a weekly and then daily basis.

Weekly

At the start of each week, look ahead at the whole week and identify the events that require you to be confident. These will be social and work related. They'll be situations like: meeting new people at a social engagement; speaking assertively when you take back an item to a shop; contributing more positively in a meeting at work; going to the doctor or dentist; telling a neighbour about something you're unhappy with; giving a presentation at work … the list is endless. Once you know what's coming up, you've already started to think and prepare mentally for it.

Fight your gremlin when it tries to convince you that these events are nightmares waiting to happen. We all have these feelings on occasions, even confident people. They won't let the gremlin get them though. You mustn't either.

Use your initiative; don't just think reactively about the week ahead. In other words, don't only focus on the events that *others* have requested you to attend and the jobs *they've* asked you to do. Think also of opportunities *you* can present yourself with. These may well be the opportunities that you would previously have dismissed outright or avoided, even though, deep down, you knew you should have seized them. Winston Churchill put his finger on it when he famously quoted, 'The optimist sees opportunity in every danger; the pessimist sees danger in every opportunity.'

So, have the courage to put yourself forward now when at work, for example, when your boss needs a volunteer to do a presentation; take a positive step when there's an opportunity to make new friends; seize the chance when you have an opportunity to learn something new. Tell yourself that no longer will you let opportunities in life pass you by. If *you* don't take them, somebody else, someone *more confident* than you, probably will. That's just not right; it's daft, it makes no sense; you can't let it happen any more.

Daily

At the beginning of each day, you'll need to psych yourself up. Just like a professional sports person prepares mentally for a match, so *you* should prepare for each day of your Self-Confidence Project. You'll need to be strict about this at the beginning, otherwise you'll forget. After a while, you'll get into the habit of thinking positively about the day ahead.

When you're trying something new (for example, one of the tips you've read in *Brilliant Self Confidence*) aim to do it for twenty-one days. Twenty-one days is the magical period of time over which you need to do something before it becomes a regular habit. Bear this in mind and try it: it really works.

Start as you mean to go on: set aside a little time, just a few minutes, at the beginning of each day. Think about the day ahead; play out in your mind each situation you're likely to be confronted with and the people involved. Of course, there will be some situations you can't foresee; there's no way of knowing they're going to happen. That's to be expected. The key is that, the better you get at dealing with the situations you *can* foresee, the more confident you'll feel when dealing with those you can't.

Minute by minute

Stay alert at all times. Your gremlin could ambush you at any time, probably when you're least expecting it to. Remember – your gremlin prefers you as you *used to be* and will be trying to hold you back. Only a positive and focused mindset will keep it at bay.

No longer are you on your own; you have your Self-Confidence Project to support you now. Have it at the forefront of your mind at all times. Push out the boundaries, have the courage to behave differently. Keep practising, keep learning and slowly but surely your confidence will grow.

Don't rush. Never panic. Take one step at a time.

'If you hear a voice within you say 'you cannot paint', then by all means paint, and that voice will be silenced.'

Vincent Van Gogh

Van Gogh may well have been referring to his gremlin.

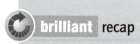 **brilliant** recap

Chapter 10

- Be sure you know how 'readily' you embrace the need to change.
- Having a flexible approach to 'change' is vital during your Project.

- 'Change' means doing some things differently to the way you used to.

- It could be to do with communicating verbally and non-verbally, thinking or behaving.

- Track your progress through the 'change process': denial, resistance, exploration, commitment.

- Plan your actions weekly, then daily; be disciplined.

- Don't rush, don't panic; take a step-by-step approach.

Conclusion: Following it through

'Even if you're on the right track, you'll get run over if you just sit there.'

Will Rogers

You've probably been trying out some of the exercises and tips you've read in *Brilliant Self Confidence*. That's great; that's exactly what you should have been doing. The road map (in Chapter 1) steered you in that direction and encouraged you to do it. If you sit still you'll be in danger of grinding to a halt.

Now think back to where we began. You'll remember Sid, my neighbour: brick by brick he built his first house. He started by clearing the ground, laying the foundations and setting the cornerstones. Having read *Brilliant Self Confidence*, you're now at this point in *your* building programme.

You've cleared away the past, built a firm foundation and you've cast five key cornerstones:

● positive mental attitude and self-discipline
● focus and direction; personal objectives and goals
● communication style; assertiveness and influence
● dealing with setbacks
● embracing change.

These cornerstones should form the heart and lifeblood of your Self-Confidence Project. They're the mainstays to building your confidence from now on; keep them at the forefront of your mind.

It took my neighbour eighteen months before he could stand proudly in front of what he'd built. It's impossible to say how long it's going to take you; everyone's different. Some people's Self-Confidence Project takes a matter of weeks, others take months, others perhaps even years.

Keep your expectations realistic. Start by setting yourself small, manageable challenges. Don't get disappointed if some things don't work out as you had hoped or planned. That's bound to happen on occasions. Remember, just as Sid learnt lessons while building his first house, so will you learn lessons building your confidence. Keep trying regardless; treat every experience as a learning experience no matter what happens. Make sure you do learn from it though, so that next time you do it better.

At some point, you'll start to feel that you're there; you've finished your Project. You'll have the self-confidence to describe yourself as a confident person! Great – *Well Done*! But stay aware, don't let yourself get complacent; your confidence levels will ebb and flow. It happens to us all, it's natural. Even the most confident people take a knock every now and then. The key is to reflect and to look positively at the experience, learn from it and move on: you have all the tools to do this now.

You've read *Brilliant Self Confidence* so you'll always have this knowledge base – your job now is to *build* on it. Don't leave the cornerstones untouched without giving them something to support. Otherwise, over time, they'll become overgrown and covered with brambles and weed. They're no good to you then; they're wasted. You built them; *now build on them*.

Just as the house was built with bricks, your Self-Confidence Project will be built with *practice*. Practice requires you to have the self-discipline to put yourself in situations out of your comfort zone; situations from which you would previously have shied away. The more you practise, the stronger you will feel and the more confident you will become.

Sometimes you'll have to curb your natural instincts; you'll have to behave differently to the way you normally behave; you'll have to adapt your style. You could even say you'll have to 'act' the right 'part' for the right situation. There's nothing wrong with that at all. It doesn't mean you're being 'false'; it means you're being *clever.*

So be disciplined, prepare well and have the courage to seize every opportunity. I wish you every success with your Self-Confidence Project.

'Tomorrow is the most important thing in life. It comes into us at midnight very clean. It's perfect when it arrives and puts itself in our hands. It hopes we've learned something from yesterday.'

John Wayne

Index

action, taking 40–1, 224
action plans 65–6, 238–40
actors 39, 143, 147
adrenalin 146–7
aggressiveness 114, 115–17, 121,
    122–3
answers, preparing 126–31,
    142–3
anxiety 146–7
apologising 45–6, 204
appearance
    dress 135, 174
    physical 10, 83, 188
Ashe, Arthur 125
assertiveness 113–50, 243
    body language 125, 145, 147–8
    event preparation 132–43
    finding a balance 114–15,
        122–3
    influence 113–14, 121, 243
    negative thinking 124–5
    preparing answers 126–31,
        142–3
    saying 'no' 127–31
    standing up for yourself 202–4
    thinking on your feet 144–6
Astaire, Fred 41
attention, commanding 166
attitude 6
    changing 12–17
    negative 44
    positive 37–43, 243
attractiveness, physical 10, 83, 188

audience 134–5, 137, 154, 167

balance
    assertiveness 114–15, 122–3
    life 181–4
Barlow, Gary 9
body language 164–75, 230
    assertiveness 125, 145, 147–8
    awareness of other people's 86,
        102
    in conflict situations 203
    distracting 164–5
    eye contact 137, 165–7, 173
    facial expressions 118, 155–6,
        172, 173, 203
    hands 170–1, 173
    negative attitude 44
    perception by others 77
    posture 77, 168–9, 173
    sitting 173
    space 173–5
    walking 169
breathing 159–60, 204
Burke, Edmund 148

Caine, Michael 39
caution, natural 229–30
change 229–41, 243
    coming to terms with 231–5
    putting into practice 235–40
childhood experiences 12–15,
    17–22
Churchill, Winston 42, 239

comfort zone 30, 231, 244–5
commitment to change 237–8
communication 92–108
  adapting your style 94, 95,
    101–8
  animated style 95, 96, 98,
    99–100, 105–6
  methodical style 95, 96,
    99–100, 106
  mirroring 102, 103, 104, 106,
    107
  paraverbal 157–64
  sensitive style 95, 96, 98,
    99–100, 104
  style chart 96–100
  style clashes 101–2, 103, 106
  up-front style 95, 96, 99–100,
    104–5
  see also body language;
    speaking
compromise 194, 199–200, 204
confirmation 155–6
conflict 192–208
  avoiding 199
  avoiding escalation 206–7
  compromise 194, 199–200, 204
  contesting versus giving in
    193–200
  dealing with difficult people
    201–7
  emotions 200–1
  fear of 207–8
Confucius 41
Cornerstone exercise 58–66
courage 56, 114, 117, 239
  dealing with difficult people
    204, 205
  overcoming shyness 210
  trying something new 139
Covey, Stephen 55
credibility 154

damage control 221–5
Darwin, Charles 229

delivery 157–64
denial 232–3, 234, 235, 236
difficult people, dealing with 201–7
Disney, Walt 39
'distant memories' exercise 23
distractions 164–5, 187
dress 135, 174

Edison, Thomas 41–2
Einstein, Albert 188
email 207
emotions 200–1, 222–3
energy 188
enthusiasm 162–4
equal terms, treating people on
    81–2
equipment, preparing 136–7
events, preparing for 132–43,
    154, 238–9
exercise 188–90
expectations, managing 42, 207,
    237
exploration 235–7
eye contact 137, 165–7, 173

facial expressions 118, 155–6,
    172, 173, 203
failure, fear of 15, 40, 233
  see also setbacks, dealing with
favourite words 156–7
fear 15, 40, 207–8, 233
  see also shyness
feedback 49, 83–5
fidgeting 171, 203
filming exercises 85–6
first impressions 175–7
fitness 188–90
focus 31, 55, 190–2, 243
Ford, Harrison 39
Frank, Anne 37
friendships 44

Gandhi, Mahatma 38, 71
GARMS principle 211–12

'ghost writer' exercise 167
Gide, André 229
goals/objectives 55–66, 133–4,
    237, 243
    strategic 29, 60–3, 66
    tactical 29, 63–4, 65, 66
greetings 46–7
'gremlin' concept 87–8, 139, 202,
    224, 235, 236, 238, 240
'guess who' exercise 172–3

habits 28–9, 38
    distracting 164–5
    favourite words 156–7
hands, using 170–1, 173
health 36, 188–9
Hillary, Sir Edmund 35
'homework' exercise 43

inferiority 79–80, 81–3
influence 113–14, 121, 243
insecurity, hiding 115, 116
interruptions, dealing with 203,
    205–6
intonation 161–2

Kennedy, Robert F. 40
Kent, University of 225

language, negative 45–9
lateness 186–7
laughing 225–6
learning
    children 14–15
    from experiences 17–22, 27–8,
        41–2, 57
life balance 181–4
Lincoln, Abraham 132
listening 97, 98, 99, 125, 144–5
'look and learn' exercise 148
Mandela, Nelson 102
meetings, preparing for 132–43,
    154
Mehrabian, Albert 147

memories, negative 26–7, 37
milestones 237
mind maps 59–60, 66, 153
'mirror image' exercise 168
mirroring 102, 103, 104, 106,
    107
misconceptions 9–12
motivation 190–2

names, remembering 176–7
negative perceptions 74, 77–81,
    94, 187
negative thinking 8, 15, 36–7, 230
    assertiveness 124–5
    eliminating 43–50
nervousness 146–7
    fast speaking 158
    hand gestures 171
    in voice 76–7, 85, 159–60
new people, meeting 16–17, 18,
    138, 175–7
'no,' saying 127–31
'no magnets' exercise 130–1
non-verbal communication see
    body language

objectives/goals see goals/
    objectives
opportunities
    missing 39, 119–20
    seizing 239
optimism 36, 239
organisation, personal 174, 184–5
over-confidence 75, 115

paraverbal communication
    157–64
parents, attitudes of 17–22
passive-aggressiveness 117–18
passiveness 114, 119–20, 121,
    122–3, 202
past experiences
    adult 22–8
    childhood 12–15, 17–22